The Sweeney To  Shock'n'Roll Show

Peter Miller
and
Randall Lewton

Samuel French — *London*
New York – Sydney – Toronto – Hollywood

ISBN 0 573 18030 X

SWEENEY TODD was first presented at Alsop Comprehensive School,
Liverpool in January 1979, with the following cast:

Lee Alderdice	Colin Jones
Andy Billinge	Timothy Joslyn
John Brightley	Stephen Lundberg
Noel Briscoe	Keith Mansfield
Christopher Brown	David Marshall
Ian Brown	John McCarthy
John Calland	Thomas Mitchell
Brian Comyns	Sean Moore
Timothy Evans	Alec Mosey
Martin Finnigan	Stephen Nelson
Ed Franklin	Mark Paterson
Gary Frew	Brian Robinson
Derek Hignett	Graham Smith
Michael Hill	Alan Spencer
James Hughes	Peter Swindells
Phillip Johnson	David Wills

and with the help of:

Stephen Barwise	Ann Joslyn
Ian Berry	Gary King
Paul Bolger	Vera Lewton
Chris Buckley	George Lucy
Douglas Cashin	David Mitchell
Robert Chambers	Alice Pedder
Ken Cridland	Alan Pevely
Chris Dawson	Stephen Quinn
David Foden	Harold Scanlan
Stephen Griffiths	Harry Weatherley
Philip Grove	Christopher Whittle
Jeff Hockenhull	Roy Williams

DRAMATIS PERSONAE

SWEENEY TODD, the Demon Barber

TOBIAS STOUTHEART, his Apprentice (who is not all he seems!)

MRS WILHEMINA LOVETT, a Pie-maker

ANGELO, her Italian Assistant

BILLY, a jolly Jack Tar

TOMMY, his Shipmate

THE AMAZING ALONZO, a Sorcerer par excellence

FOOZLE, the Sorcerer's Apprentice

ORLANDO, the Sorcerer's Faithful Hound

POLICE CONSTABLE, a Bobby or Peeler

BEAUJOLAIS PICKLE, brother of Branston, Gin Palace Proprietor

QUEEN VICTORIA, Monarch of the Realm

HRH's ATTENDANT, possibly Gillie Brown of Balmoral

NAPOLEON BEDLAM, Keeper of the Madhouse at Peckham

GROVEL, waiter at the Gin Emporium

GILBERT, an AGA (aged gin addict)

The OPERATOR of the Pastriacci Pie-making Machine Mark III

A HECKLER, who meets with a fitting end

A young and pretty PICKPOCKET

A bored NEWSBOY

and numerous MADHOUSE KEEPERS and INMATES, NEWSBOYS, GHOSTS, CITIZENS of London, short POLICEMEN and two VICTIMS ..... from the audience!

The action takes place in Victorian London

ACT I	ACT II
Sc.1 Fleet Street	Sc.1 Fleet Street
Sc.2 Inside the Barber Shop	Sc.2 The Bakehouse
Sc.3 PICKLE's Gin Palace	Sc.3 The Madhouse at Peckham
	Sc.4 Fleet Street
	Sc.5 The Bakehouse

THE SWEENEY TODD SHOCK 'N' ROLL SHOW·

ACT I

Scene 1   Fleet Street

MUSIC 1 Sinister music. A single spotlight reveals TODD's shop door USR. A CITIZEN enters DSL crosses the stage. As he passes the shop he rubs his chin as if he is in need of a shave, decides to go in, enters shop. Pause. Suddenly there is a very loud scream. The spot snaps out.

After a short pause bright lights come up to reveal a busy street scene; MRS LOVETT's Pie Shop USL, TODD's Barber Shop USR.

MUSIC 2   If You're of a Nervous Disposition

Off stage (handwritten)

CITIZENS	If you're of a nervous disposition, If a horror story makes you shriek. If Crippen, Hyde and Jack the Ripper scare you Our show tonight will make your knees go weak.
	(several NEWSBOYS run on from L and R)
NEWSBOYS	Shock! Horror! Hold the front page! Revelations! Villains low! Shock! Horror! Public outrage! A fearful and barbaric show!
CITIZENS	We tell a tale of blood and gore and terror Of a wretch who cared for neither man nor God. Who kept a grisly, grim and gruesome secret, A vile, vicious villain - Sweeney Todd!
ALL	Shock! Horror! Hold the front page! Revelations! Villains low! Shock! Horror! Public outrage! A fearful and barbaric show!
CITIZENS	This Sweeney Todd acquired a taste for murder. His business grew on theft, deceit and lies,

} dance (handwritten)

With his partner working in the neighbouring pie
                     shop,
The customers might eat or fill the pies!

So be prepared for shock and consternation.
If you faint when you see blood you'd better go.
If you've brought your Granny, send her round
                   the alehouse,
Then you'll be welcome to our horror show!

ALL   Shock! Horror! Hold the front page!
Revelations! Dealings low!
Shock! Horror! Public outrage!
A fearful and barbaric.
Cheerful, atmospheric,

Off stage   Tearful and hysteric
Show!

(CITIZENS gradually exit going about their business
until only one CITIZEN and a young girl PICKPOCKET
are left on stage. The PICKPOCKET looks up and
down the street then lets out a blood-curdling yell
and falls to the ground. The CITIZEN rushes over
to her.)

PICKPOCKET Aaaaaah!

CITIZEN 1   Whatever is the matter? Let me help you. Where
is the pain?

PICKPOCKET Oh! oh! Here, ah!

CITIZEN 1   (bending over her) This is terrible! Let me help
you up. There's a doctor just along the street.

PICKPOCKET (straightening) No, no. It's all right. The pain's
easing now. Just one of my turns. I'm perfectly
all right now.

CITIZEN 1   Are you sure?

PICKPOCKET Yes, yes. Thank you kindly, sir.

(The CITIZEN leaves, PICKPOCKET examines the

wallet and watch she has stolen. As another CITI-
ZEN enters she doubles up again. CITIZEN 2 rushes
to help.)

(louder than before) Aaaaaaah!

CITIZEN 2   Heavens preserve us! Allow me, madam. What
ails you?

PICKPOCKET   Aaaaaaaaaaaaaaaah! (jerks and twitches)

CITIZEN 2   (kneeling) Courage, madam. Wait here, I will
fetch a doctor.

PICKPOCKET   (jumping up) No need, sir. I assure you I am well
now.

CITIZEN 2   The lord be praised. I thought you were done for,
my dear lady. A miracle indeed, madam.

(CITIZEN 2 leaves the stage. The PICKPOCKET
again examines what she's stolen. SWEENEY TODD
enters DSL, PICKPOCKET goes into same routine.)

PICKPOCKET   (louder than ever) Aaaaaaaaaaaaaah!

(She performs a long series of jerks and twitches
with accompanying shrieks and groans. TODD
stands and watches. Finally the PICKPOCKET lies
still, exhausted.)

TODD   Is something wrong?

PICKPOCKET   Oh the pain!

TODD   Oh, I see. A pain. (walks away)

PICKPOCKET   Oh, sir. Help me for the love of God.

TODD   (turning) I do little for the love of God, girl.

PICKPOCKET   If you could just help me to my feet, sir.

TODD   You are a tiresome person. Oh, very well.

	(TODD lifts the PICKPOCKET to her feet. She starts to walk away feeling in her pockets for her loot and looks angrily at TODD who is holding up a watch. She walks up to TODD and is about to speak when he silences her with a glare.)
PICKPOCKET	(aside) Curses! I know this man. It is Sweeney Todd. I sense that he is a greater villain than I. (exit DSR)
TODD	A foolish girl to try and pick the pocket of Sweeney Todd. Yes, I am Sweeney Todd, the finest barber in London town. Here is my establishment. Note the inscription. It is in Latin. I am also a great scholar. Freely translated it reads 'Hair today, gone tomorrow'. My little joke, you know. MY LITTLE JOKE, YOU KNOW! But I have no time to waste talking. It's time that my shop was opened. You will see that my razor is as sharp as my wit!
	(He goes into the shop. TOBIAS enters wearily DSR carrying a bundle on a stick and sinks to the ground in front of TODD's shop. A NEWSBOY enters USL, his head buried in a paper. He trips over TOBIAS.)
NEWSBOY	You clumsy oaf!
TOBIAS	I am sorry. I was so weary that I could not take another step. I have walked for three days to reach London.
NEWSBOY	Hardly seems worth it. What did you want to come here for?
TOBIAS	It is a long and tedious story.
NEWSBOY	Oh well then .....
TOBIAS	But if you insist I will tell you the whole tale.
	(A violin plays mournfully in the background - sound effects department. The NEWSBOY yawns and leans against convenient wall.)

Until last week I lived a good and happy life in -
(local district). Since my father died when I was a
baby my mother and I have lived in a simple way.
We were poor but we were honest. Alas our honesty
did not protect us from our evil landlord. We were
thrown out to fend for ourselves in the cold, cruel
world. My mother was overcome by the shame of
our situation, took ill and last Thursday evening -
oh, I weep to think of it - she died in my arms.

NEWSBOY   (awaking from doze) Yes, well ... (starts to leave)

TOBIAS   Before she died .....

                 (NEWSBOY leans on wall again.)

                 ..... she gave me this. (produces banknote) It
                 was all she had, and she told me to seek an appren-
                 ticeship here in London.

NEWSBOY   And I hope you .....

TOBIAS   For three days, an orphan, I trudged on weary feet
                 through mud and foul weather until I reached this
                 place. I have had nothing to eat, little to drink and
                 my clothes are rags. I can go no further - and I'm
                 only little.

NEWSBOY   You are starving, are you? You have a five pound
                 note there. Buy yourself a dinner with that.

TOBIAS   No! This banknote is all I have in the world. I
                 must keep it as long as I can. If I spend this then
                 I am doomed to poverty and starvation.

NEWSBOY   I'd keep that money in your pocket if I were you.
                 There are some funny characters about, you know.
                 Well, I wish you luck mate. (makes a quick exit)

TOBIAS   (to audience) There is more to my story than I
                 dared to tell a stranger. ('he' removes cap to
                 reveal beautiful long hair) The world is a danger-
                 ous place for a young girl, alone, without a friend
                 or protector. This disguise has deceived all those

whom I have met on my journey and now I hope it
will enable me to find a home and earn a living ....
(she replaces the cap tucking in hair) ... although
I must confess I am at a loss to know where to begin
my search. I am lost and weary and the wind stings
through these ragged clothes. I started my journey
with strength and a confident heart but now .... now
..... I think constantly of my poor mother and my
heart grows heavy.

(She sobs. TODD opens his shop door to see who is
making the noise, sees TOBIAS and walks out and
hits him.)

TODD   Be quiet! You squealing bundle of rags. Are you
trying to drive away all my customers? (aside) I
have few enough as it is.

TOBIAS   Forgive me, sir. (looks at the shop) You are a
barber, sir?

TODD   A barber? The finest barber in London. In the world

TOBIAS   An honest trade which I would be proud to learn.

TODD   What do you mean, boy?

TOBIAS   If you should need such a thing as an apprentice,
sir, I would be a credit to you, sir, I promise you,
sir, if you would take me on, sir.

TODD   (aside) He is a weak and miserable specimen. Yet
I might find him useful. My last apprentice is .. er
.. no longer with me. Tell me, boy, what is your
name? Who are your parents?

TOBIAS   My name, sir, is Tobias Stoutheart. My parents,
alas sir, are dead.

TODD   (aside) This is good. And tell me, boy, what you
would have to offer me as my apprentice?

TOBIAS   I am strong, sir, hard-working, sir, diligent, sir,
keen, sir, enthusiastic, intelligent, careful, quick

to learn and full of energy, sir.

TODD   (aside) Yecchh! I could not stand such a boy. No,
              boy, I find I do not need an apprentice. (walks away)

TOBIAS   And I have money to pay for my education, sir.

              (She holds up the banknote. TODD dashes back and
              grabs it.)

TODD   But your story has touched my heart. I will take
              you on. I happen to have the articles of apprentice-
              ship here.

              (He brings out a piece of paper which unfolds to
              reach from his hand down to the floor and hands
              TOBIAS a pen.)

              Here, sign here. Never mind reading it, just sign.

              (TOBIAS signs.)

              (aside) Now I have him.

              (TODD kicks TOBIAS.)

              That is just a sample, boy, of what you will get if
              you do not do as you are told. You have signed the
              articles. From now on you will not breathe without
              my permission. Do you understand?

TOBIAS   Yes, Mr Todd.

TODD   Yes, Mr Todd, sir.

TOBIAS   Yes, Mr Todd, sir.

TODD   Now get inside and get to work.

TOBIAS   (entering shop) .... and I'm only little.

TODD   (to audience) I suppose you feel sorry for the
              wretch? Do you think kindness is of any use? Would
              I be where I am today if I had been kind? No! Cruelty

is the way and I enjoy it so. But look at the time -
and still no customers.

(ALONZO enters DSL carrying an enormous case
bearing the words 'THE AMAZING ALONZO'. He
puts down the case and looks at the shops.)

Aha! This looks like a likely customer. Well
dressed - wealthy perhaps - and a stranger to these
parts. I always reserve a warm welcome for stran-
gers. I will prepare something special for him.

(TODD goes into the shop. ALONZO looks back the
way he has come on.)

ALONZO   (impatiently) Foozle! Oh confound the boy! Foozle!

(FOOZLE enters DSL dressed in ill-fitting and out-
rageously multi-coloured clothing. He is carrying
a dog lead on the end of which is an empty collar.)

FOOZLE   Yes, sir. Just coming, sir.

ALONZO   (despairingly) Foozle! Oh, how are the mighty
fallen! That I, the Amazing Alonzo, illusionist
extraordinaire, who have journeyed through the lands
of the Arabian nights and mastered all the necroman-
tic arts of the mystic east, should sink so low as to
be plagued with an imbecile such as this. (puts his
hand to his brow)

FOOZLE   (aside) Doesn't he speak lovely?

ALONZO   Look boy! Look in your hand. What do you see?

FOOZLE   Nothing, sir. (looks more closely) No, I tell a lie
it's - uggh! (wipes his hand on his coat)

ALONZO   The other hand, simpleton.

FOOZLE   (looking at the empty collar) Er?

ALONZO   Vacuous villain! Where is Orlando?

FOOZLE   Don't worry, sir. He will be close by. I expect he
                    felt like a bit of exercise. A lady dog perhaps, if
                    you know what I mean, sir?

                    (ALONZO stares coldly at him.)

                    A lamp-post perhaps. I'll go and find him, sir,
                    shall I? Yes, I shall. Won't take a minute, sir.

ALONZO   It is unnecessary, fool. He approaches. Fortunately
                    he is more intelligent than his keeper.

FOOZLE   Here, Orlando! Here, boy!

                    (ORLANDO bounds on, runs around, licks both of
                    them and sits beside ALONZO.)

ALONZO   Ah, Orlando! You bring back doleful memories. To
                    think that you and I have enchanted the crowned heads
                    of Europe with our sorcery. Archdukes and kings
                    have begged me to reveal the secrets of my wizardry.
                    An audience. If only there were an audience here I
                    would ....

                    (FOOZLE looks at the audience.)

                    ...... show you wonders, Foozle.

FOOZLE   Well, actually, sir......

ALONZO   Miracles I could perform, my boy, but without an
                    audience what purpose would there be?

FOOZLE   But look, sir.

                    (He points to the audience but ALONZO does not look.)

ALONZO   Should I waste my incantations upon the empty air?
                    A conjuror without an audience is like a ....

FOOZLE   Look, sir.

                    (ALONZO looks.)

An audience.

(ALONZO steps to the edge of the stage and inspects the audience.)

ALONZO   Foolish child! That is not an audience. It is a rabble.

FOOZLE   I wouldn't say that, sir.

ALONZO   Of course not. You are even more ridiculous than they are, but Orlando knows. I have performed before much greater audiences than this.

(ORLANDO nods in agreement.)

But no, no, you must not beg me to perform an illusion.

(FOOZLE wasn't going to.)

(louder) You must not beg me to perform an illusion..... Well, if you insist. Let me see, what species of illusion would appeal to an audience such as this?

(ORLANDO barks.)

You are right, of course, my faithful hound. My most elementary trick will please their simple minds. Foozle - the receptacle.

FOOZLE   Eh?

ALONZO   The hat!

(FOOZLE takes a bowler hat out of the case.)

For this illusion I will need the assistance of a member of the audience - you sir, perhaps. Yes, you sir, with the asinine expression. Thank you. Step up here please.

(From the audience VICTIM 1 appears. It is VERY important that the VICTIMS should be cast members.)

Would you hold the receptacle, sir?

(VICTIM 1 takes the hat.)

Foozle, the ingredients.

(FOOZLE produces a jug full of disgusting, sticky goo from the suitcase.)

Thank you. Examine the receptacle, sir. No hidden compartments?

VICTIM 1   No. (gives hat back)

ALONZO   Observe. (pours the goo into the hat) And now, sir, I am about to test your courage and determination. Close your eyes. I have here a gold sovereign. It is yours, sir. All you have to do is, without opening your eyes, put on the hat.

VICTIM 1   But ..... (opening eyes)

ALONZO   A gold sovereign, sir. Close your eyes and take the hat.

(ALONZO cleverly substitutes another hat. He can involve ORLANDO in the substitution if desired but it is important that FOOZLE does not see what has happened. VICTIM 1 takes a deep breath and with a quick movement puts on the hat. ALONZO, with a flamboyant gesture approaches him and lifts up the hat. A large amount of confetti falls from inside.)

Voila!

(VICTIM 1 reaches for the gold sovereign but it is pocketed by ALONZO, who is encouraging applause.)

VICTIM 1   But .... What about .....?

ALONZO   (pushing him back to his seat) A big hand for the gentleman, please.

FOOZLE   That was terrific. Can you do another?

ALONZO   My tricks are wasted on this riff-raff. I am in need
                of a shave. I will leave Orlando in your charge.
                Meet me at six o'clock at the Gin Palace in Smith-
                field. (aside) Yes, to my eternal shame, I have
                fallen victim to the demon drink. Oh misery!
                (entering shop) Hello there. I say, fellow! Barber!

FOOZLE   (looking intently at the hat) Yes, I think I see.....
                Ladies and gentlemen, you are lucky tonight to be
                present at the first performance of the Great Foozle!
                I need a volunteer from the audience. Ah, the very
                man!

                (VICTIM 2 is brought on stage from audience.)

                Thank you, sir. You saw this trick just now.

VICTIM 2   I did.

FOOZLE   Right then. Cop hold of that.   (hands him hat)
                Oh, sorry. (takes hat back and imitates ALONZO's
                tone) Would you please examine the receptacle ....
                and now the ingredients. (pours more goo into hat)
                And now if you will take the receptacle, please sir.
                I am about to test your courage, your determination.
                Close your eyes, sir.

                (VICTIM 2 does so eagerly.)

                If you can now put on the hat, I have here .... I have
                here ..... (searches his pockets) I have here half
                a bacon sandwich. It could be yours. Courage, sir.
                Put on the hat.

                (Before VICTIM 2 can do so, ALONZO comes out of
                the shop.)

ALONZO   Foozle! What are you doing to this poor old gentle-
                man? I'm so sorry, sir. Please excuse my assis-
                tant. Very sorry.....

                (He guides VICTIM 2 back to his seat.)

                I will deal with the boy severely, I assure you.

(FOOZLE sneaks off.)

Where has he gone? And confound this barber! There
is not a sign of the man. Orlando! Has he left you
here alone? That boy suffers from terminal incompetence. Wait there, Orlando. I will try once more
to arouse this barber.

(He turns and bumps into TODD in the doorway.)

TODD   Forgive me, sir. I have been detained. Certain
              preparations were necessary for a satisfactory - er
              - execution on your throat.

ALONZO   Indeed, sir, I become daily more accustomed to
              feckless inefficiency.

TODD   Thank you, sir. Step inside please. I will be with
              you in one moment.

(ALONZO enters shop.)

'Certain preparations.' Ha ha haaaaa! His clothes
suggest that he is worth a sovereign or two. His
suit alone will fetch a guinea. Ha ha haaaa! Oh,
sometimes I'm so rotten I can't stand it. Ha ha!

(ORLANDO growls.)

What's that? Get away from here you flea-bitten
mutt. Get away, I say!

(He kicks ORLANDO who cringes and howls. As
TODD turns away ORLANDO attacks him from behind.
There is an enormous fight but ORLANDO is chased
off.)

If there are two things I hate - animals ..... and
people. You know sometimes I look in the mirror
and I say, 'Sweeney, how did you ever become so
deliciously evil?' Evil. I love the sound of the word.
Evil! Evil! Evil!!! Ha ha haaaaaaaa!

(Green lights come up as MUSIC 3 begins.)

I'm Evil!

I'm evil.
I'm wicked. I enjoy it.
I'm evil.
All virtue I'll destroy it.

There's not a shop in London town
(Throughout the trade it's known),
Can polish off a customer
As quickly as my own!

I'm evil.
My wit is razor sharp.
I'm evil.
Soon he'll be playing on a harp.

I'm evil.
You really have to laugh.
My razor
Will saw this conjuror in half.

There's not a shop in London town
(Throughout the trade it's known),
Can polish off a customer
As quickly as my own!

It's shocking
How much I cherish sin.
He's waiting
Now I shall go and do him in!

(TODD is about to go into a spectacular dance but is
interrupted by shouts from offstage.)

ANGELO   (off) Signore! Signore!   (rushes on in an agita-
ted state) Signore! Signore!

(TODD ignores him.)

Signore! Signore!

(ANGELO tugs TODD's sleeve.)

TODD Take your macaroni-stained fingers off my coat!
What is it you want?

ANGELO Signore Todd. My mistress, Signora Lovett, she
wisha you piss.

TODD (giving him a look) Peace. She wishes me peace.
You mangle the English language with your Neapoli-
tan nonsense. What is it you want?

ANGELO Oh, Signore Todd. Angelo - is a me - have a da
important message from Signora Lovett. Is a very
important.

TODD Well?

ANGELO Is a very important.

TODD I know 'is a very important', but WHAT IS IT?

ANGELO I forget.

(TODD raises his fist.)

I remember.

(MRS LOVETT enters USL behind ANGELO.)

TODD Well?

ANGELO She tella me .... she tella me ....

(He catches sight of MRS LOVETT and is thrown into
a panic.)

Ah, Signora Lovett ... I remember .... I remember

(MRS LOVETT approaches threateningly.)

You say .... no wait ... I remember .... Don't hit
me ..... Signora .... per favore ... aiuto ... ohh!

(ANGELO is now sandwiched tightly between TODD
and MRS LOVETT. He sinks to his knees. MRS LOVETT

takes hold of one ear and gestures towards the other.)

MRS LOVETT   Mr Todd?

(TODD takes the other ear and they lift ANGELO to his feet.)

I have a kind heart, Mr Todd.

TODD   Indeed, Mrs Lovett.

MRS LOVETT   I have been like a mother to this boy, Mr Todd.

TODD   I have often thought so, Mrs Lovett.

MRS LOVETT   He is Italian you know, Mr Todd.

TODD   I had an inkling, Mrs Lovett.

MRS LOVETT   It was my kind heart that led me to take him in. He was penniless, starving. He had stowed away in a ship bound for London. When he arrived here he knew not a word of the language. I found him lying in the gutter not fifty yards from this very spot. Who knows what might have become of him if I had not taken him in?

(ANGELO is standing on tiptoe, his ears still firmly held by TODD and MRS LOVETT.)

TODD   Who indeed?

MRS LOVETT   And yet despite my kindness, my generosity, my .. ... er ...

TODD   Your magnanimity?

MRS LOVETT   The very word ... my mahogany. Despite all this the boy is ungrateful.

TODD   Surely not.

MRS LOVETT   Sadly yes.

ANGELO	Plis signora....
MRS LOVETT	He is workshy.
ANGELO	No signora.
MRS LOVETT	Si signora. If you will excuse me, Mr Todd.

(TODD releases his ear. MRS LOVETT leads ANGELO to the edge of the stage and kicks him back to her shop.)

Back to the bakehouse. See to the ovens. The latest batch of my delicious pies should be nearly ready. Speaking of the shop, Mr Todd.....

(She makes sure ANGELO has gone into shop.)

I find myself a little short of ... er ... pie filling, Mr Todd.

(Nudge, nudge, wink, wink.)

TODD	Why do you not speak to the butcher, Mrs Lovett.
MRS LOVETT	(aside) The barbarous villain plays games with me! No butcher can supply me with meat of the quality my customers have come to expect.
TODD	Your customers. Ah yes. Indeed, I see a bigger throng about your door each day. Your business is expanding and to think that I can remember when you first went into the pie business. You were finding it difficult to make both ends meet (meat). (aside) I will make her sweat.
MRS LOVETT	(aside) He tries my patience. You know my meaning!
TODD	Now understand my meaning. I have a fresh supply of meat. (gestures to his shop door)
MRS LOVETT	How fresh?

TODD　　　　　Not yet slaughtered. But there has been a slight increase in my prices. Inflation, you know.

MRS LOVETT　How much?

TODD　　　　　Double.

MRS LOVETT　You ... you ... Sir, we had an agreement!

TODD　　　　　(aside) We never meet but like gunpowder and fire there is an explosion!

MRS LOVETT　I have been a fool to fall in with your murderous schemes. Yet what can I do? Without your 'meat' my pie shop would be ruined. My customers are mad for my 'veal' pies. They worship my gravy. If only they knew what they were eating. I have no alternative, Mr Todd. I will pay your price.

TODD　　　　　There is money for both of us in this, my friend.
　　　　　　　　(aside) She is no friend of mine!　(together)
MRS LOVETT　(aside)　He is no friend of mine!

TODD　　　　　If my share is greater than yours, it is because my part of the work is more hazardous.

MRS LOVETT　Spare me your fatuous explanations, Mr Todd. You force me against my will to perform all manner of evils.

TODD　　　　　Force you, Mrs Lovett? Come now, confess. Do you not feel the slightest satisfaction in your work?

MRS LOVETT　What an idea!

TODD　　　　　Be truthful. Is there not a tingle of pleasure that comes with each evil deed?

MRS LOVETT　Well, er ....

TODD　　　　　Yes?

MRS LOVETT　YES! I do enjoy it! Why should I pretend otherwise? Sometimes I look at myself in the mirror and I say,

'Wilhemina Lovett, how did you ever become so mag-
nificently wicked?'

(Lights dim, they cackle. MUSIC 4 starts.)

We're Evil!

TODD &   We're evil!   *Song*
MRS LOVETT   We're nasty and we're mean.
                We're evil!
                We make a gruesome team.

                There's not a shop in London town
                (It's not within their powers)
                Can bake or sell a hot meat pie
                With gravy such as ours.

                We're rotten
                We murder and we steal.
                We butcher!
                In the pies we call it veal!

                We're nasty.
                Murdered corpses by the ton.
                It's ghastly,
                But we have a lot of fun!

                There's not a shop in London town
                (It's not within their powers)
                Can bake or sell a hot meat pie -
                If they knew the truth we bet they'd die.
                Can bake or sell a hot meat pie -
                We think you know the reason why.
                Can bake or sell a hot meat pie
                With a gravy such as ours!

                I'm evil!
                S/he's evil!   *go to shop*
                We're evil!

(Exeunt with a final horrifying cackle.   MRS LOVETT
to her shop and TODD to his. As they go two sailors
enter DSL. BILLY is young and handsome, TOMMY is
older with a thick beard and a parrot on his shoulder.)

TOMMY   What do you think of London, Billy, on your first
                visit? Wonderful, isn't it?

BILLY   'Wonderful' I expect that's the word for it, Tommy.

TOMMY   You'll enjoy it, Billy. With all the wealth we have
                after our voyage you'll find you're a very popular
                character in this fair city. I will show you all the
                sights, starting with the gin palace of my old friend,
                Beaujolais Pickle, where we will find sweet liquor
                and good company. Let's waste no more time, I'm
                developing a thirst.

BILLY   I am not a drinking man, shipmate, as you know,
                but I will join you for an hour for friendship's sake,
                and then I must journey on. To think that in a few
                short hours I shall see again the face of my beloved
                Susan.

TOMMY   She must be a rare sweetheart for your passion to
                survive a voyage of such length.

                (During the following speech the sounds of seagulls,
                waves, ship's rigging and stirring nautical music
                are heard, slowly increasing in volume.)

BILLY   I have been three years at sea and in all that time I
                have heard but once from Susan. She has been a
                mainstay to me in all weathers. I have been roused
                from my hammock, dreaming of her, for the cold,
                black, middle watch. I have walked the deck, the
                spray beating in my face, but Susan was at my side
                and I did not feel it. I have been reefing on the yards
                in cold and darkness, when I could hardly see the
                hand of my next messmate but Susan's eyes were on
                me and there was light. When 'land' was cried from
                the masthead I seized the glass. My shipmates saw
                the cliffs of England - I, I could see but Susan. I
                leapt upon the dock, my shipmates find hands to grasp
                and lips to press - I find not Susan's...... (by now
                he is shouting to be heard over the sound effects)....
                But tomorrow as the dawn kisses the fields of Kent,
                I shall kiss the lips of the fairest flower in England -
                my Susan. (sound effects end abruptly)

TOMMY   (waking from a daydream) Sorry. What did you say?

(Sound effects begin again.)

BILLY   I have been three years at sea . . . .

TOMMY   (cutting across, sound effects stop) We're wasting good drinking time, shipmate. Come - to the gin palace.

BILLY   I will join you shortly but first I must buy for my dearest Susan the gift that I have promised her on my return.

TOMMY   A gift?

BILLY   I promised to place round her exquisite throat a string of pearls which would match the beauty of her fair skin.

TOMMY   A string of pearls?

BILLY   Sometimes I wonder if I'm talking to you or the parrot. Yes, a string of pearls. Look, I have . . . .

(ANGELO enters USL from Pie Shop and sees the sailors. He is full of admiration.)

. . . . . . copied these lines from a book of poetry.
'The hours I spent with thee, dear heart,
Are as a string of pearls to me.
I count them over every one apart,
My rosary.'

ANGELO   (aside) Ah sailors! How I woulda love to joina da navy. I sail to here from Italy and all I see isa da inside ofa da lifeboat, but now I wish to see da beauties of da world. Bellissima . . . .

(TOMMY and BILLY come over to him.)

. . . . . . to have a signorina ina every port.

BILLY   You are right, lad. A good uniform works its way
                with the women.

TOMMY   It's a grand life in the navy.

ANGELO   Will you tell me, signore, of your life in the navy?

TOMMY   Sing the lad your song, Billy.

BILLY   Stow it, Tommy. I am no singer.

TOMMY   No singer! Bless you, lad. Whenever we want to
                catch a mermaid, we only make Billy sing a verse
                and we've twenty round the ship. Less of your mod-
                esty. Sing for the lad.

BILLY   Oh, very well, but you'll have to help me out.

                MUSIC 5   We Love the Navy

BILLY &   When we were lads sitting on our mothers' knees
TOMMY   We dreamed of a life sailing on the seven seas.
                Now that we're grown we have sailed the whole
                                                    world wide,
                From Liverpool to Hong Kong, from Wapping to
                                                    Port Said.

                We love the Nav-ee,
                The swell of the sea.
                Travelling free,
                We run with the tide,
                We sail side by side,
                The stars are our guide.

TOMMY   If you're small or sickly, if people pick on you,
                Sign on for naval training. You'll find what they say
                                                    is true,
                Soon you'll have muscles strong as iron, nerves like
                                        steel and suntanned skin.
                They'll be no girl that you can't charm, no fight
                                        that you can't win.

BILLY &   We love the Nav-ee,
TOMMY   The swell of the sea.

> Travelling free,
> We run with the tide,
> We sail side by side,
> The stars are our guide.

BILLY

> If you're a lad who is keen to see the world,
> Then hoist up your anchor, let your mainsail be
>   unfurled.
> Cast off and set a course to find horizons new,
> To see wonders that lie hidden from all but a
>   chosen few.

BILLY &
TOMMY &
ANGELO

> We love the Nav-ee,
> The swell of the sea.
> Travelling free,
> We run with the tide,
> We sail side by side,
> The stars are our guide.

(They have been performing a complicated dance
involving all the traditional sailors' duties - hauling
ropes, climbing the mast, keeping a lookout etc.
During the last chorus ANGELO attempts to join in
causing them to become entangled with each other.
All three exit DSR repeating chorus as they go. The
lights dim and a large notice is carried across the
stage - 'MEANWHILE'.)

Scene 2   Inside TODD's shop

(ALONZO is sitting in the chair USC. TOBIAS is
mixing the shaving soap. TODD is sharpening his
razor. Some levers are on the wall USR, door USL.)

ALONZO

Devil take you, sir. You are the slowest barber it
has ever been my misfortune to meet.

TODD

Nay, sir. I will very soon polish you off. Ha haaa!

(His laugh is so loud and horrifying that TOBIAS
drops the bowl of shaving soap.)

Give me that. You shall pay later for your clumsi-
ness.

ALONZO   Come, sir. My beard has grown another inch while I have sat here in the chair.

TODD   Coming, sir, coming. Tobias, step around the corner and find the time on St Dunstan's church clock while I finish this gentleman off.

TOBIAS   It is ten o'clock, sir. I have just heard it strike.

TODD   Oh .... well, Tobias, run along to Mr Woolworth's store and collect the razor I left there to be sharpened.

TOBIAS   It is here, sir. He brought it himself not ten minutes since.

TODD   Very well, Tobias. Go to Mistress Tesco's modern emporium and purchase a dozen of her delicious muffins.

TOBIAS   But, Mr Todd, there are two plates of muffins in the parlour. You cannot require more.

TODD   TOBIAS! Never mind the time, disregard the razor, abandon the muffins, but GO, DEPART, RETIRE, WITHDRAW, TAKE YOUR LEAVE, MAKE TRACKS ......

(Hitting TOBIAS with every word.)

...... SLING YOUR HOOK!

TOBIAS   I think I'll go now, if you don't mind. (aside as she leaves) This is strange behaviour. And it's not fair - I'm only little.

TODD   Now, sir, your shave.

ALONZO   Never in my considerable experience of establishments throughout the length and breadth of Europe, nay the world, have I had the misfortune to meet a barber of such monumental incompetence, such ....

(TODD gives him a mouthful of soap.)

TODD   That has stopped your mouth, sir, and now I shall
                        stop it permanently.

                        (With a grand gesture he slits ALONZO's throat
                        laughing madly.)

                        But there is no time to waste. I must dispose of
                        the evidence. The lever.

                        (He goes to the levers on the wall USR and pulls one.
                        The lights go out.)

                        Wrong lever!

                        (Lights come on again and he selects a second lever.
                        The chair disappears through the wall. There is a
                        long falling sound and a thud. TODD laughs madly.)

                        Now to see what this ill-tempered conjuror was
                        worth.

                        (He exits USL and the chair returns to its original
                        position as TOBIAS enters DSL from street.)

TOBIAS   (going over to the chair and kneeling down to inspect
                        the trap/secret door) This is curious. What is the
                        purpose of this trap-door?

                        (TODD enters USL with a pile of clothes, sees TOB-
                        IAS and throws the clothes back through the doorway.
                        Creeps up on TOBIAS from behind.)

TODD   What are you doing, boy?

TOBIAS   (leaping up) Nothing, Mr Todd.

TODD   Why were you kneeling on the floor?

TOBIAS   I .. er .. just tripped, Mr Todd.

TODD   Tripped? (aside) Does he suspect?

                        (He grabs TOBIAS threateningly.)

Be warned my inquisitive young friend. It would be
most unwise, most unwise, for you to repeat a word
of what passes in this shop, or dare to make any
supposition or draw any conclusion from anything
you see or hear, or fancy you see or hear. Do you
understand me? Eh? Eh?

TOBIAS   (terrified) Yes, sir. I won't say anything, sir.

(TODD moves away.)

If I as much as say one word, sir, I wish I may be
made into veal pies at Mrs Lovett's next door, sir.

(TODD freezes in his tracks.)

TODD   How dare you mention veal pies in my presence!
                   (aside) I think I shall have to polish the boy off.

(TODD is about to kill TOBIAS then and there when
the street door opens DSL and ORLANDO bursts in.
He runs around and barks madly at the chair. TODD
tries to kick him and falls over.)

Tobias! Don't just stand there. Catch hold of the
pestilential animal.

(TOBIAS does so.)

Now take him to the river - and throw him in!

(ORLANDO howls.)

With a stone tied around his neck!

TOBIAS   But sir ....

TODD   Do as I say!

TOBIAS   Yes, sir.

(Exit DSL dragging ORLANDO with him.)

TODD   Cursed animal. And the magician, for all his fine

words had precious little of value on his person. Perhaps his clothing will fetch a price. (picks up clothes
from doorway USL) Let me see. This cloak is of
good quality and the shirt is of fine material,too, but
what is this? Curse you,Sweeney Todd, for a clumsy
fool! Blood! Here - and there. Damnation! I dare
not let these be seen. They are fit only for the furnace. No money! Worthless clothing! This magician
has played a last trick even in death. Yet his body
will, I am sure, be of use to my grisly pie-maker
neighbour. I should meet no problems with that sale.
But Sweeney,you must learn from this mistake. Trust
in the chair, Sweeney. Ay, the chair. Why slit throats
and spill blood when a long fall and a broken neck will
do the job with less sanguification?

(BILLY enters from street door DSL. TODD quickly
hides the clothing.)

Good morning, sir. Can I help you?

BILLY   Good morrow, friend. I have need of your craft. Let
               my hair be cut at once for tomorrow I have to meet a
               lady.

TODD   You have come then to the right establishment. The
               finest barber shop in the city.sir. Please sit down.
               You're not a Londoner yourself, sir?

BILLY   No, I return to the village of my birth tonight.

TODD   You have been at sea, sir?

BILLY   Yes. I have only lately come up the river from an
               Indian voyage.

TODD   A great distance, sir.

               (TODD steps back in amazement as he notices the
               string of pearls in BILLY's pocket. He walks forward
               and addresses the audience.)

               I can scarcely believe my eyes. Can it be a string of
               pearls that hangs from his pocket? (going back)

Pardon me, sir, but can that be a string of pearls
that hangs from your pocket?

BILLY   What? Oh yes, indeed. I am glad you spoke of it.
In confidence let me tell you, they are of the value
of twelve thousand pounds. I must be more careful.

TODD   Yes, there are some wicked people in this city. You
would hardly believe how wicked. But sit back, sir,
and relax. Close your eyes. It will all be over before you know what has happened.

(BILLY sits in the chair and shuts his eyes. TODD
goes USR and pulls the lever. BILLY screams as he
disappears.)

This is better. A string of pearls and a fine new
naval uniform. I must let Mrs Lovett know that I
have two carcases for her attention. I must see to
the body.

(Exit TODD USL. TOBIAS enters from the street
DSL with a POLICE CONSTABLE.)

TOBIAS   (entering) My master does not seem to be here at
present, sir. I will tell him you wish to speak with
him.

CONSTABLE   Don't trouble yourself young man. I will await his
return.

(The CONSTABLE wanders round inspecting the shop.)

TOBIAS   (aside) To lie is a wicked thing but I must lie to my
master. I could not bring myself to drown the dog.
I set him free in the park. He will not trouble my
master further.

(TODD returns carrying the pearls and the sailor's
uniform. He doesn't notice the CONSTABLE and
TOBIAS. He holds up the uniform.)

TODD   (pleased) Not a stain.

CONSTABLE   Mr Todd?

                 (TODD jumps in the air with fright. He throws the
                 clothes on to the table by the door. TOBIAS goes USL
                 to inspect them.)

TODD   Yes ... er ... I am Sweeney Todd.

CONSTABLE   (taking out his notebook) I would like a word with you.

TODD   Er ... yes?

                 (TOBIAS holds up the uniform.)

TOBIAS   He is dead, sir.

                 (TODD turns in terror.)

TODD   What? NO! What do you mean?

TOBIAS   (surprised) The dog, sir. You instructed me to kill
                 him. He is dead, sir.

TODD   Ah, the dog! Of course, the dog, yes. He is dead.
                 (to CONSTABLE) The dog. Dead. The dog - dead.

CONSTABLE   Yes, sir. As I understand it the dog is dead, sir?

TODD   Yes.

                 (He snatches the clothing from TOBIAS and throws it
                 through doorway USL.)

                 You wanted to speak to me?

CONSTABLE   Yes, Mr Todd. On the subject of theft, Mr Todd ....

                 (TODD finds he still has the pearls in his hand and
                 stiffens, bundling them out of sight.)

                 ... and murder, Mr Todd.

TODD   (picking up razor) Theft? MURDER!?

CONSTABLE   As I was passing down the street, in a southerly
                   direction, at fifteen minutes past midnight, this very
                   morning, Mr Todd....

TODD   Yes? (aside) What has he seen? My heart misgives.

CONSTABLE   Your front door was unlocked. You could have been
                   robbed, Mr Todd. You could have been murdered in
                   your bed.

TODD   Oh! Oh, I see. Well, thank you, constable. I will
                   be more careful in future. Thank you very much.

                   (He pushes CONSTABLE to the door.)

CONSTABLE   (as he leaves) Theft, Mr Todd. Murder, Mr Todd.

TODD   (to TOBIAS) Murder, Mr Todd. Murder, Mr Todd!
                   I will murder you, bringing a policeman in here.
                   What do you mean by it?

TOBIAS   Mean, Mr Todd?

TODD   Yes, very mean! I am famous for it! You shall see
                   how mean I can be!

                   (He approaches TOBIAS threateningly.)

TOBIAS   (aside) It's not fair this, you know. I'll be black
                   and blue by the interval - and I'm only little!

                   (TODD and TOBIAS move to opposite sides of the
                   stage as MUSIC 6 begins.)

                   I'm Only Little

TOBIAS   When I first came here I had my doubts.
                   I cannot please him, he screams and shouts.
                   He kicks and beats me and more besides,
                   I'm only little - but it hurts my pride!

                   I'm only thirteen but every day
                   My skin is ageing, hair turning grey.
                   I'm poor, I'm lonely, nowhere to hide,
                   I'm only little - no one's on my side!

I thought he'd help me, my life he'd save.
I signed a paper - became a slave -
But was he honest? Now you decide,
I'm only little and I could have cried!

TODD

I'll have to kill him
he stirs my bile.
It aggravates me
to see him smile.
It won't look like murder
but suicide.
He's only little -
but troublesome besides.

TODD &
together
TOBIAS

This irritating creature has no respect. And the secrets of my business he may detect If he ever knows he will certainly expose me. I see it in my nightmares Does he suspect?	But this must end soon I have it planned. For I'll not take it - I'll make a stand. My sense of duty shall be my guide, I'm only little - but I'm big inside!
I'll have to kill him he stirs my bile. It aggravates me to see him smile. It won't look like murder but suicide. He's only little - but troublesome besides.	Mournful sighs, plaintive cries. Are my senses telling lies? Fearful moans, Hopeless groans, Creeping from the cellar stones.
This irritating creature - Does he suspect?	I'm only little - But I'm big inside

DSL

(TODD begins to beat TOBIAS but is interrupted by MRS LOVETT entering DSL.)

TODD

Get out, boy! GET OUT! (pushes him off DSR)

MRS LOVETT

Mr Todd, I have been insulted.

TODD

That Italian brat up to his tricks again?

MRS LOVETT   No. I have locked <u>him</u> in the bakehouse. I fear he may begin to understand the evil nature of the work he performs. I shall keep him in future under lock and key.

TODD   How then have you been insulted?

MRS LOVETT   Through Her Majesty's Post Office, Mr Todd. (waves letter in the air) They have insulted me. They have dared to ask for my rent.

TODD   No!

MRS LOVETT   They have. They demand £40, Mr Todd.

TODD   £40! How long is it since you paid?

MRS LOVETT   Well .... let me see .... not long .... er ... three, four .... no, it must be five .... yes ... five years.

TODD   Ha ha haaaa! So they have finally caught up with you!

MRS LOVETT   I'm glad you're amused, Mr Todd, as it is you who will have to pay.

(TODD chokes.)

Be sure if I am arrested for debt, Mr Todd, there may be others who will be as sorry as I. Do you understand me?

TODD   You dare to demand money from me? (aside) I see she too will have to be polished off.

HECKLER   Ah shut up!

(The HECKLER should be in the balcony if there is one or at the back of the audience. If there is a balcony two seats will need to be occupied by the HECKLER and the dummy. HECKLER stands.)

TODD   Who said that?

HECKLER   I did, up here. You're rubbish. Get off.

TODD   (shading his eyes) Who is it? Brian Clough?

MRS LOVETT   It could be the drama critic from the Gazzelle (local paper).

HECKLER   Let's see somebody who can act. Bring the dog back
                on.

MRS LOVETT   (to TODD) Keep him talking.   (runs off stage)

HECKLER   That's right. Come back when you're sober.

TODD   Everybody has the right to be stupid, sir, but you
                abuse the privilege.

HECKLER   I don't know which is worse. your acting or your
                singing. As for him playing the piano - as a pianist
                he'd make a good ratcatcher.

TODD   Now listen, my man, these people have paid good
                money to come in here tonight.

HECKLER   How much do they have to pay to get out?

                (This can continue with references to local events and
                personalities for as long as is necessary for MRS
                LOVETT to make her way to the balcony or the back of
                the audience. She dashes in shouting:)

MRS LOVETT   Right you! Out! Come on!

HECKLER   Who's going to make me?

                (There is a furious fight. The HECKLER is finally
                vanquished and either thrown over the balcony - the
                dummy having been cunningly substituted - or if there
                is no balcony, MRS LOVETT pushes her way through
                the audience, drags out the HECKLER , hits him on the
                head and throws him to the floor.)

MRS LOVETT   (shouting to TODD) That's dealt with the rowdy ele-
                ment. What do you think?

TODD   Veal and ham by the look of him.

MRS LOVETT   How about my money, Mr Todd?

TODD   We will discuss it later. I will meet you this evening
                  at the gin palace of Beaujolais Pickle.

exit?

                  (MRS LOVETT leaves. The 'body' is removed. TODD
                  holds up the pearls in a spotlight DSC.)

                  When a boy, the thirst of avarice was first awakened
                  by the fair gift of a farthing; that farthing soon be-
                  came a pound; the pound a hundred, so to a thousand,
                  till I said to myself, I will possess a hundred thou-
                  sand. This string of pearls will complete the sum.
                  Ha ha haaaaaa!

                  (The curtains close on TODD's demoniacal laughter.
                  FOOZLE enters in front of curtains carrying case.)

FOOZLE   (looking left and right) Ah, excuse me, sir. This
                  looks like a good opportunity..... If you would re-
                  turn to the stage, sir.

                  (VICTIM 2 does so, and FOOZLE takes the hat and
                  jug out of the case to repeat trick   but,just as the
                  VICTIM 2 is about to put on the hat he is tapped on
                  the shoulder by the POLICE CONSTABLE.)

CONSTABLE   'ello, 'ello, 'ello. What's goin' on 'ere then?

FOOZLE   Just a little trick, officer.

CONSTABLE   (taking hat from VICTIM 2) Do you have a licence as
                  a street performer?

FOOZLE   Well ... er .... no.

CONSTABLE   Well, I shall have to ask you to move along,please.
                  Come along, don't dawdle. And you, sir, please.
                  (peering closely at VICTIM 2) Haven't I seen you on
                  one of my wanted posters? You're not the Finsbury
                  Flasher, are you? No? Well, move along then please.
                  I'm sure I've seen him somewhere.

                  (As FOOZLE, the CONSTABLE and VICTIM 2 leave the
                  stage the curtains open for the next scene.)

Scene 3 PICKLE's Gin Palace

(The scene is one of great activity and noise. The
stage is set with a great many tables and stools, the
bar is USR with a door to the street USL. Most of
the CUSTOMERS are well on the way to passing out.
CHILDREN sit on the floor drinking what they can
steal from the tables. BEAUJOLAIS PICKLE, the proprietor is rushing about from table to table with large
jugs labelled 'GIN'. He is assisted by GROVEL,his
waiter. There are two 'special' tables at opposite
sides of the stage DSR and DSL. TOMMY is sitting at
the DSR one.)

CUSTOMER 1   Pickle! Pickle! Where is the man? Pickle!

PICKLE   Yes, sir. Coming, sir. More gin, sir?

CUSTOMER 1   No! I will have wine. There is some demon in my
heart that leaps at the sound of the word. The mon-
ster's up and wine, wine alone, can satisfy it.

PICKLE   Grovel! Come here at once, Grovel.

(GROVEL dashes over.)

GROVEL   Yes, sir.

PICKLE   Grovel, wine for this customer.

GROVEL   (throwing back his head) Owooooooooooo!

(CUSTOMER 2 staggers to the centre.)

CUSTOMER 2   Gentlemen .... and ladies, a toast. The Queen!

(All the CUSTOMERS stand and raise their glasses.)

CUSTOMERS   The Queen!   (drink and sit in perfect unison)

CUSTOMER 2   Oh what a perfect world would this be if all the green
fields were tobacco and all the rivers gin! (coughs
disgustingly and staggers back to his seat)

PICKLE   Indeed, sir. It is a most refreshing liquor. How
                      would we manage without it in these sad and troubled
                      times? It strengthens the spirit, improves the health,
                      broadens the mind .....

                      (CUSTOMER 3 leaps to her feet.)

CUSTOMER 3   LADIES and gentlemen! The Queen!

CUSTOMERS   (rising as before) The Queen!   (drink and sit
                      in perfect unison)

CUSTOMER 4   (struggling to his feet) The QUEEN!   (falls flat
                      on his face and is ignored by everyone except the
                      CHILDREN who go through his pockets)

TOMMY   I wonder what has become of my shipmate. It is
                      late. He should have met me long since. He would
                      not fail. I hope he has not met with some accident.

CUSTOMER 1   Come, let's have a song!

CUSTOMER 3   (who fancies herself a bit of a prima donna)Mr Pickle,
                      we will sing the praises of your entrancing, enrap-
                      turing and enchanting liquor. Let us sing, ladies and
                      gentlemen - to gin!

CUSTOMERS   (rising) To gin!

                      MUSIC 7   Gin!

PICKLE   If your breath is short or if your eyes are dim -
CUSTOMERS   drink gin!
PICKLE   If exhausted or weak in the head or limb -
CUSTOMERS   try gin!

GROVEL   Don't believe them when they tell you it's a sin -
CUSTOMERS   not gin!
GROVEL   If you feel temptation, don't resist, give in -
CUSTOMERS   to gin!

ALL   Gin! Gin!
                      We'll always love it right or wrong.
                      Gin! Gin!

The inspiration for our song.
Gin! Gin!
Your servants we will always be.
Gin! Gin!
A kind of liquid poetry!

BOY 1   It makes no difference how young you begin -
CUSTOMERS   with gin.
GIRL 1   It's a friend who'll stick with you through thick & thin
CUSTOMERS   is gin!

CUSTOMER 1   You can drink it if you're fat or if you're thin -
ALL   good gin.
CUSTOMER 1   It will bring a healthy glow to every skin -
ALL   will gin!

ALL   CHORUS

CUSTOMER 2   It's on sale in every pub and bar and inn -
ALL   fine gin.
CUSTOMER 2   It's the reason for old Gilbert's foolish grin -
ALL   is gin!

CUSTOMER 3   Drink it from a glass, a bucket or a bin -
ALL   drink gin.
CUSTOMER 3   Tell the waiter to fill right up to the brim -
ALL   with gin.

ALL   CHORUS

CUSTOMER 5   If you choose it you can bet you'll always win -
ALL   on gin.
CUSTOMER 5   Your eyes will blur, your knees go weak, your head
                                                       will spin -
ALL   with gin!

(CUSTOMER 5 is very drunk and staggers about un-
able to carry on with the next two lines. There is a
moment of confusion as he is helped to a seat then
everyone launches into the chorus:)

ALL   Gin! Gin!
We'll always love it right or wrong.
Gin! Gin!

The inspiration for our song.
Gin! Gin!
Your servants we will always be.
GIN! GIN!
A KIND OF LIQUID POETRY!

(As the song ends there is a total collapse on the
floor and GILBERT who has not taken part in the song
comes forward to the centre. He is at least two
hundred years old, bent double and using a stick.)

GILBERT   Waha! Weedolberingle. Gerasticleecontertiblust.

(He laughs eccentrically – it is not necessary for
GILBERT to stick too rigidly to the script!)

CUSTOMER 1   (rising from floor) Yes, yes, Gilbert. Ha ha!

(CUSTOMERS all look at each other mystified. They
all climb back to their seats. GILBERT sits with
great difficulty at the table with TOMMY. FOOZLE
enters USL carrying case with ORLANDO following.)

FOOZLE   At last. It's taken me hours to find this place. It
is almost six o'clock now. The Amazing Alonzo
should be here soon. (sees ORLANDO) Orlando!
I thought you had stayed with my master.

(ORLANDO nods.)

You did? Is he here then?

(ORLANDO shakes his head.)

Where is he then?

(ORLANDO runs to the door USL and comes back.)

What do you mean?

(ORLANDO takes FOOZLE's coat tails in his mouth
and pulls.)

Stop it! I'm not going anywhere. It's cold out there

and in here it's warm and comfortable. (looks around) Well, it's warm anyway. (sits at table DSL)

(ORLANDO whimpers mournfully.)

Waiter, bring me something to warm me on this chill night.

GROVEL	Gin? Brandy? Rum? Wine? Champagne?
FOOZLE	Er .....
GROVEL	Claret? Port? Whisky? Stout?
FOOZLE	Have you got any cocoa?
GROVEL	One mug of cocoa, sir. Yes, sir. Anything else?
FOOZLE	Yes, the dog could do with a drink, too.
GROVEL	Yes, sir.
CUSTOMER 1	Gentlemen! The Queen!
CUSTOMERS	(rising) THE QUEEN! (sit in unison)

(GROVEL brings drinks for FOOZLE and ORLANDO.)

FOOZLE   (tasting drink) What game are you playing? This is water. (throws it at GROVEL)

GROVEL   I beg your pardon, sir.

(GROVEL takes the dog dish from ORLANDO and pours the contents into FOOZLE's mug.)

GILBERT   (to TOMMY) Gureegooberindipolikgingle, atakabol.

(CUSTOMERS 1 and 3 gather round as he speaks.)

CUSTOMER 1   Oh aye, Gilbert.

CUSTOMER 3   Always one for a jest, eh Gilbert?

TOMMY   Er .... excuse me ... what did he say?

CUSTOMER 3   Oh bless you, sir. No one has understood a word
                 Gilbert has said for the past fifteen years.

GILBERT   Gabble, babble, gabble.   (laughs uproariously,
                 the others join in)

CUSTOMER 2   (rising) Ladies and gentlemen! The Queen!

CUSTOMERS   (rising) THE QUEEN!

                 (GILBERT has joined in and as everybody sits in
                 unison so he falls over. He is carried out, still
                 bent double, legs in the air.)

CUSTOMER 1   Come on, Gilbert. Time you were in bed. Give us
                 a hand with him, Charlie.

                 (CUSTOMERS 1 and 5 bump into TODD in the entrance
                 USL as they carry GILBERT out.)

TODD   Out of my way, ruffians!

PICKLE   Welcome, Mr Todd.

TODD   (ignoring him) Waiter! Bring me wine! Quickly
                 fool!

                 (He walks over to TOMMY's table DSR, points over
                 TOMMY's head. TOMMY turns round. From under
                 his coat TODD produces a 'RESERVED' sign which he
                 places on the table.)

                 Excuse me, I think you are sitting at my table. If
                 you wouldn't mind.....

                 (TOMMY is puzzled but leaves and crosses to table
                 DSL where FOOZLE is sitting.)

                 I see my mutinous partner in crime is late once
                 again. I become more and more impatient with her
                 snivelling cowardice but,more important - she is
                 becoming a danger to me. I shall have to make plans

for her disposal.

CUSTOMER 3   (rising) Ladies and gentlemen! The Queen!

CUSTOMERS   (rising) THE QUEEN!

                (They all sit in unison having toasted, including
                TODD who is very patriotic. TOMMY returns to
                the table DSR.)

TOMMY   Excuse me. It is Mr Todd, I believe. Mr Sweeney
                Todd, the barber?

TODD   Indeed that is my name and trade. What business
                have you with me?

TOMMY   It is late. Your shop is closed?

TODD   No, I'm there now shaving a customer. Of course
                it is closed!

TOMMY   This is curious, sir. My shipmate, Billy, was to
                meet me here as soon as you had dealt with him.

TODD   (standing and addressing audience) Dealt with him?
                Indeed I have dealt with him. Ha ha haaaaaaa!
                (returning to TOMMY and sitting) I know nothing of
                your friend, sir. I have shaved no sailors today. Do
                not bother me. (turns away)

TOMMY   (going DSL) You are most uncivil, sir. Good even-
                ing to you. (aside) Something seems to whisper in
                my ear that this fellow knows of my friend's fate.

CUSTOMER 2   (rising) Gentlemen! The Queen!

CUSTOMERS   (rising) THE QUEEN! (all sit in unison)

                (FOOZLE crosses to TODD, ORLANDO follows.)

FOOZLE   Mr Sweeney Todd, I believe?

TODD   I have that honour.

FOOZLE   My master, the Amazing Alonzo ... (points to
                name on the case, TODD starts) ... visited your
                shop this afternoon. He arranged to meet me here
                at six. I wonder if he gave you any idea as to his
                plans after he left your shop?

TODD   (stepping over to audience) Left my shop? Little
                does the poor fool know his master never left my
                shop. Ha ha haaaaaa!

                (As he returns to the table ORLANDO snaps at him.)

                Curse this confounded dog! It plagues me.

FOOZLE   You know the dog?

TODD   (quickly) Know it? How should I know it? What do
                you mean? Be gone! You weary me! (aside) That
                cursed boy Tobias has disobeyed me once too often!

FOOZLE   (returning to table DSL) I will not stay where I am
                not welcome. (aside) This behaviour is most sus-
                picious!

Back of   (MRS LOVETT enters and joins TODD at table DSR.)
stage

TOMMY   (to FOOZLE) I noticed that you were speaking to
                Mr Sweeney Todd.

FOOZLE   Yes, indeed. You know, it is most curious ......

                (Their conversation becomes inaudible and inter-
                spersed with that of TODD and MRS LOVETT.)

MRS LOVETT   Perhaps I find you in a better humour in the company
                of your thieving companion here?

                (TODD looks around.)

                (tapping the bottle) This gentleman here. He robs
                people of their brains, their digestion and their con-
                science - to say nothing of their money. Speaking of
                which, Mr Todd, as I told you earlier I am in urgent
                need of £40.

TODD   Ah, yes, the £40.

MRS LOVETT   (aside) If I ply him with drink, I may get it out of
                him..... Allow me to fill your glass, Mr Todd.

TOMMY   (to FOOZLE) You amaze me, sir. My situation is
                almost identical. My companion ....

MRS LOVETT   (to TODD) I have some inkling, Mr Todd, of the
                wealth you have acquired through your evil trade.
                £40 is nothing to a man of your means. Come sir!

TODD   Say no more, Mrs Lovett. The money is yours.
                Here, I have it upon me now.   (takes wallet out
                and gives her £40)

FOOZLE   (to TOMMY) My suspicions increase with every
                word you speak. I believe we should join forces.

TOMMY   Let us wait and follow this curious barber.

FOOZLE   You are right. We must have evidence before we act.

MRS LOVETT   (to TODD) Another drink, Mr Todd? I am over-
                whelmed by this change of heart. A gift of £40!

TODD   (aside) She will not live to spend it. Ha haaaaaaa!

CUSTOMER 1   (rising) Gentlemen! The Queen!

                (CUSTOMERS all stand.)

                No! No! You misunderstand me. Gentlemen - the
                Queen!

                (To the amazement of all QUEEN VICTORIA enters
                with ATTENDANT. CUSTOMERS all fall to their knees
                and grovel.)

VICTORIA   My subjects, we are pleased with your welcome.
                You grovel beautifully. You may rise - respectfully.

                (They do so. PICKLE enters DSL with some more
                wine. He does not notice VICTORIA.)

PICKLE   Here you are, sir, and though I say it myself, there
                  ain't a better bottle opened at Buck House.

VICTORIA   At <u>Buckingham</u> <u>Palace</u>, sir, one uses this substance
                  for the shampooing of the Royal Corgis.

PICKLE   (throwing himself on the floor) Oh, forgive me,
                  your Majesty.... I did not notice you there.

VICTORIA   You did not notice us! Are you blind, sir? Does
                  not our magnificence fill the room? We are most
                  insulted by your words.

PICKLE   Oh, your Majesty!

                  (He grovels even more. GROVEL enters DSR.)

GROVEL   Are you all right, Mr Pickle? Who's the old crow?

VICTORIA   Ooooooh!

                  (She faints and is caught by her ATTENDANT.)

PICKLE   Oh, Grovel, be quiet. Oh your Majesty forgive him.
                  Grovel, come here. This is Her Gracious Majesty
                  Queen Victoria.

                  (GROVEL is impressed.)

                  Well don't just stand there, Grovel. Grovel.

GROVEL   Grovel grovel?

PICKLE   Yes, grovel Grovel!

                  (GROVEL grovels.)

VICTORIA   (recovering) Oh this is really insufferable! One
                  knew one would hate these new-fangled walkabouts.
                  One should never have listened to that unspeakable
                  Mr Gladstone.

PICKLE   May I welcome you to my humble establishment,
                  your Majesty. I am Beaujolais Pickle.

VICTORIA	We sympathise. We knew your brother, Branston.
PICKLE	Might I ask the reason for your doing me the honour of visiting my humble, lowly, modest er ... paltry er ....
VICTORIA	Insignificant?
PICKLE	..... insignificant establishment?
VICTORIA	We are following the advice of our Prime Minister, Mr Gladstone. We are advised that we should try to improve our image. We are attempting to win back the affection of the British Public.
CUSTOMER 3	Ladies and Gentlemen! The Queen!
CUSTOMERS	(toasting) THE QUEEN!
VICTORIA	We are pleased. We remarked to Mr Gladstone that our image was in excellent condition but the irritating fellow insisted on our putting on these clothes and visiting the haunts of some of the lower orders, the common people, the slum-dwellers and the riff-raff, the vulgar herd, the great unwashed, the humble, the servile and the base.
PICKLE	(sincerely) Oh, thank you, your Majesty.
GROVEL	Most kind, most kind.
TODD	Ladies and Gentlemen, let us pay tribute to our most gracious and noble Queen and to the glorious empire over which she rules. May I say, your Majesty, in the words of your distinguished grandfather – 'Born and educated in this country I glory in the name of Briton.'

(VICTORIA is escorted to a seat by TODD as they all cheer.)

MUSIC 8   Queen and Empire

TODD	Drink, drink a health to the Queen.

          Drink and toast the Empire.
          Drink to Britain standing supreme.
          OTHER NATIONS RETIRE!

VICTORIA   Drink, drink a health to me.
          Drink and toast my Empire.
          Drink to Britain noble and free,
          Other nations admire.

MRS LOVETT   On British strength and British skill
          The world is pleased and proud to lean;
          And in far-flung lands the natives thrill
          To the name of our great and glorious Queen!

ALL   Victoria, Victoria,
          Victoria, Victoria,
          Your Empire long shall last!
          Victoria, Victoria,
          Victoria, Victoria,
          Your beauty is unsurpassed!

TODD   The world is full of beauties rare,
          Of mountains grand and valleys green.
          But no earthly splendours can compare
          With those of our own magnificent Queen.

ALL   CHORUS

          (TODD stands on chair and recites the poem. The
          CUSTOMERS etc. hum the tune in the background.)

TODD   This country bears a world known name
          Though it is but a little spot.
          I say 'tis first in the scroll of fame
          And who shall say it is not?
          Of the deathless ones who shine and live
          In arms, in arts, or song,
          The brightest the whole wide world can give
          To this little land belong.
          'tis the star of earth, deny it who can
          The island home of an Englishman.

MRS LOVETT   In heaven's eye who can deny
          That Britain stands and stands alone,

In pride of place the supreme race
All others are in shadow thrown.

ALL   CHORUS

(During the final part of the song Union Jacks
appear in every possible corner of the stage. They
sprout from the walls and hang from the ceiling.
Everyone on stage waves at least two. A patriotic
tableau is formed with VICTORIA as its centre-piece.)

ALL   On yonder height what golden light
             Triumphant shines and shines alone?
             Unrivall'd blaze! The nations gaze!
             'tis not the sun, 'tis Britain's throne.

             On which the sun,   on which the sun,
             On which the sun,   on which the sun,
             On which the sun,   the sun, the sun,
             The sun, the sun,   the sun, the sun,
             On which the bright and glorious
             Queen Victorious,
             Bright and glorious,
             Queen Victorious
             Su-un
             Never sets!

             BLACKOUT

             MUSIC 9 Rule Britannia

             (A spirited rendition plays as the curtains close.)

             END OF ACT ONE

ACT II

Scene 1   Fleet Street

MRS LOVETT's Pie Shop USL, TODD's Barber Shop USR. Stage is bare.
After a moment MRS LOVETT comes out of the shop and hangs a notice
on the door: 'NEXT BATCH OF PIES READY IN TEN MINUTES'. The
CITIZENS come on in ones and twos. They look at the notice and at
their watches. MRS LOVETT goes back into Pie Shop.

MUSIC 10   Pies!

CITIZENS   If you want to know the reason for our sighs –
                                        it's pies!
                When we say we love them we aren't telling lies –
                                        love pies!

CITIZEN 1   When this aroma's in the air my stomach cries –
CITIZENS   for pies!
CITIZEN 1   They're delicious in whatever shape and size –
CITIZENS   are pies!

CITIZENS   Pies! Pies!
                We'll always love them right or wrong.
                Pies! Pies!
                The inspiration for our song.
                Pies! Pies!
                A finer feast you never saw.
                Pies! Pies!
                We eat them and we cry for more!

CITIZEN 2   Our devotion to their taste we can't disguise –
CITIZENS   these pies!
CITIZEN 2   You should follow our example if you're wise –
CITIZENS   eat pies!
CITIZEN 3   Their superiority no one denies –
CITIZENS   meat pies!
CITIZEN 3   To sing their praises hear our voices rise –
CITIZENS   these pies!

CITIZENS   CHORUS

(CITIZEN 4 has a hysterical fit and falls to the floor.
The others crowd round her. MRS LOVETT sticks her
head out of the shop door. No one sees her.)

MRS LOVETT   The customers are gathered round like flies -
                                    for pies.
                  But for each new batch another victim dies -
                                    my pies!

(She goes in and brings out a tray of pies which she
sells during the following verse.)

CITIZENS   She's an addict; you can see it in her eyes -
                                    for pies.
                  She can't give them up no matter how she tries -
                                    these pies!

(They eat pies and sing a final chorus at the same
time, spraying the stage and the first three rows
with crumbs.)

                  Pies! Pies!
                  We'll always love them right or wrong.
                  Pies! Pies!
                  The inspiration for our song!
                  Pies! Pies!
                  A finer feast you never saw.
                  Pies! Pies!
                  We eat them and we cry for more!

CITIZEN 1   Mrs Lovett, your meat pies are the finest I have
                  ever tasted.

CITIZEN 2   I would give a lot to know the recipe for your deli-
                  cious gravy.

MRS LOVETT   Oh, ma'am, that is a well kept secret indeed.   Crowded

CITIZEN 3   What I like about your pies is that they have so much round
                  ..... so much ... so much body in them.   me

(MRS LOVETT gives him a look.)

CITIZEN 4   (laughing) Perhaps - perhaps that - perhaps that is the secret ingredient - bodies.

(They all laugh uproariously. MRS LOVETT looks most alarmed.)

CITIZEN 1   Is that your dark secret, Mrs Lovett?

(They all laugh again. MRS LOVETT decides to make the best of it.)

MRS LOVETT   I see I am beaten, my friends. Indeed you have hit upon it. My pies indeed contain ... human flesh.

(They all laugh heartily.)

Yours, sir, contains a portion of my mother-in-law.

(Louder laughter.)

And yours, ma'am, certain pieces of the late Arch-bishop of Canterbury.

(They are by now screaming with laughter.)

Dance

MUSIC 11   <u>Secret Recipe</u>

MRS LOVETT   I'd been making pies for twenty years -
CITIZENS   years.
MRS LOVETT   My business though was not a great success,
                 Then I made a change that ended all the sneers -
CITIZENS   sneers.
MRS LOVETT   And now to you my secret I'll confess.

                 It ain't veal, it ain't steak, it ain't ham,
                 You'll never guess.
                 It ain't beef, it ain't pork, it ain't lamb,
                 It's human flesh!
                 And now my secret recipe
                 Has made a wealthy woman of me,
                 'cos everyone's into my pies -
                 Everyone's into my pies!

MRS LOVETT   For years I tried experiments with pastry -
CITIZENS   pastry.

MRS LOVETT	I made it short and flaky, choux and puff. Then I thought of how to make the meat more tasty -
CITIZENS	tasty.
MRS LOVETT	And now my clients just can't get enough!
ALL	CHORUS
MRS LOVETT	So now I've solved my old financial problem -
CITIZENS	problem.
MRS LOVETT	Pie fillings come here on their own two feet, And once inside, of course, I kill and rob them -
CITIZENS	rob them!
MRS LOVETT	They meet their maker and then I make meat!
ALL	CHORUS
CITIZENS	She'd been making pies for twenty years - *lie on*
MRS LOVETT	years! *backs*
CITIZENS	Her business, though, was not a great success. Then she made a change that ended all the sneers -
MRS LOVETT	sneers!
CITIZENS	And now to you her secret she's confessed!
ALL	CHORUS

(MRS LOVETT goes back into her shop and the CITI-
ZENS leave the stage. TODD enters from his shop
and speaks to the audience:) *go back to shop*

TODD   Gathering clouds warn the mountaineer of the approa-
ching storm. Let them now warn me to provide against
danger. I have too many enemies to be safe. I will dispose of them one by one until no evidence of my guilt
remains. My first step must be to stop the babbling
tongue of Tobias Stoutheart. Mrs Lovett, too, grows
scrupulous and dissatisfied. I've had my eye on her
for some time and I fear she intends mischief.

(TOMMY, FOOZLE and ORLANDO enter USL behind
TODD.)

A little poison skilfully administered may remove
any unpleasantness in that quarter. Ha ha haaaaa-
(laugh is cut off, hears noise behind) Who's there?

FOOZLE	Sweeney Todd! Where is my master?
TODD	How should I know, imbecile?
TOMMY	Sweeney Todd! Where is my shipmate?
TODD	Why do you ask me, you nautical nitwit?

(ORLANDO barks at TODD.)

Be gone, you overfed whippet!

(ORLANDO attacks TODD.)

Get him off me. Why do you dog my footsteps?

(ORLANDO and TODD fight.)

How dare you hound me in this way! (fight continues)

TOMMY   I am in no doubt that this man has committed some unspeakable crime.

FOOZLE   I fear, friend, that our companions may be dead.

TOMMY   If that be so may I not see salt water again if I do not bring this man to justice. Let us bide our time. We must find evidence to support our suspicions.

FOOZLE   Orlando! Come!

(ORLANDO stops attacking TODD.)

Be sure, sir, that you will not continue with your evil plans.

TODD   Ha ha haaaaaa! Who shall stop me?

FOOZLE   If Heaven gives me power, I shall.

(Exit TODD laughing hysterically to MRS LOVETT's shop. TOMMY, FOOZLE and ORLANDO exeunt DSR.)

BLACKOUT

Scene 2 The Bakehouse in MRS LOVETT's cellar

(It is dark and spooky. A table with drawer USL,
a piece of wall with a hidden entrance USR next to
a door leading to the ovens, and a large piece of
machinery draped in sacking USC.Door to shop DSL.
MRS LOVETT drags ANGELO on DSL.)

ANGELO   Oh, signora, why you kip me lockeda ina da cellar
                here?

MRS LOVETT   Stop whining, boy. We have work to do.

ANGELO   Not more pies!

MRS LOVETT   Yes, of course more pies. Business is very good
                today. Fetch me the latest batch from the ovens.

                (Exit ANGELO USR.)

                It seems the boy does not yet suspect anything. I will
                keep him under lock and key to be sure.

                (ANGELO returns in distress, carrying a pie.)

ANGELO   Ooooh, signora! Isa hot!   Here, signora!

                (He hands the hot pie to MRS LOVETT.)

MRS LOVETT   Don't give it to me, fool. Ow! (hands it back)

ANGELO   (running around madly) Ow! Ooooh! Signora!

                (ANGELO throws the pie from one side of the stage to
                the other. MRS LOVETT catches it, DSR.)

MRS LOVETT   Ow! Open that drawer, quickly!

                (ANGELO turns and opens drawer in table USL.
                MRS LOVETT runs over and drops the pie into the
                drawer. Drawer has no bottom and the pie crashes
                to the floor.)

                Fetch the cool pies from the bakehouse, stupid boy!

(Exit ANGELO USR. MRS LOVETT clears up the mess. ANGELO returns with an enormous stack of pies ten feet high which wobbles alarmingly.)

Be careful, boy!

(ANGELO runs around the stage almost tipping the pies on to MRS LOVETT and the audience. Finally he can maintain the balance no longer and the stack slowly tips over towards MRS LOVETT. Just before it hits the ground MRS LOVETT catches the top pie and she and ANGELO hold the stack between them.)

Take them to the shop!

(ANGELO tucks the stack under one arm and takes them out DSL. MRS LOVETT yawns.)

I'm not getting enough sleep. If only I could sleep - without dreaming.

(ANGELO returns.)

Now we must prepare the next batch of pies.

ANGELO   (groaning) Is a no end to the work. Avanti vermicelli ....

MRS LOVETT   (grabbing him by the ear) What do you say, boy? Am I not a kind and considerate employer?

ANGELO   Si signora. (released) Rigatoni spumanti!

MRS LOVETT   (giving him a look) I am such a kind and considerate employer that I have purchased at enormous expense - £40 - a new invention from your own native land which will revolutionise the pie-making industry - here!   (uncovers the large piece of machinery USC) The Pastriacci Pie-making Machine Mark III!

ANGELO   Oh signora! E bellissima!

MRS LOVETT   And beautiful, too.

ANGELO   How does it worka?

MRS LOVETT   I have the instruction booklet, here. This is where
                    you will be useful. The instructions are all in Italian.
                    You must translate.

ANGELO   (taking the book, reads:) 'IMPORTANT NOTICE —
                    The makers accept no responsibility for any injuries
                    or deaths which may occur as a result of using the
                    Pastriacci Mark III.'

MRS LOVETT   Never mind that! What is the first thing we have to
                    do?

ANGELO   The firsta thing it say .... 'Plug it in'.

MRS LOVETT   Plug it in? Plug it in?! What are you talking about?
                    Have you no sense of time? It is 1853!

ANGELO   (looking at his watch) No, signora, it isa ten past
                    nine. It say here, signora, 'plug it in'.

                    (MRS LOVETT shrugs and plugs it in.)

MRS LOVETT   Right. What's next?

ANGELO   'Put in the ingredients'.

MRS LOVETT   The ingredients. Ah, yes....   (picks up a large
                    bag labelled 'FLOUR' and throws it in the top of the
                    machine - bag and all) Fetch some water, Angelo.

                    (ANGELO exits DSL. Whilst he is gone MRS LOVETT
                    produces a 'human' leg and other items on a tray
                    from the bakehouse and throws these in. ANGELO
                    returns with a jug of water - not necessarily full -
                    which is poured into the machine from the side.)

                    Now what?

ANGELO   'Select your programme.'

MRS LOVETT   'Programme'?

ANGELO   Si signora. On the dial here. You choose-a the
                size of the pie.

MRS LOVETT   Ah, yes. A medium size one, I think. Right. Next?

ANGELO   'Switch on'.

MRS LOVETT   (doing so) Switch on.

                (Dials whirl. An extraordinary bubbling and fizzing
                noise is heard. A pie shoots out of a hole in the
                machine - not the side on which they are standing -
                and smashes on the floor.)

ANGELO   (reading) 'Be a ready to receive the pie at window A!

MRS LOVETT   Now you tell me! Look at that!

ANGELO   Try again, signora. Press the switch.

MRS LOVETT   Press the switch. (she hurries to window A - this
                time the pie shoots out of the top and hits her on the
                head) I should have known better than to buy an
                Italian machine. It takes after you. It doesn't work!
                (kicks the machine angrily)

ANGELO   (still reading) Warning! Never - repeat never -
                kicka da machine!

                (The machine begins to work, a few pies shoot out of
                the holes in the sides and one comes out of the top. It
                builds up to a crescendo of weird noises and an enor-
                mous explosion. The machine falls apart revealing
                the OPERATOR inside, black-faced and singed looking.
                He walks over to MRS LOVETT carrying a bag of flour,
                and snatching book from ANGELO reads:)

OPERATOR   'Garibaldi risorgimento minestrone suppa inglese.'
                You no read? Never - repeat-a never - kicka da
                machine!

                (He dumps the bag of flour on MRS LOVETT's head
                and storms out DSL.)

MRS LOVETT   (coughing) This is all your fault. Clean up this
               mess.   (exit DSL)   *DSL*

ANGELO   (picking up pies and putting the machine back to-
               gether) Oh how I wish I was back in Napoli - the
               wine, the musica, the sunshine .... the spaghetti!
               Zis place I am bullied. It isa miserable life. See,
               here ina da cellar there is nothing visible buta da
               darkness. I think it woulda be quite unbearable if
               it wasn't fora da delicious odour ofa da pies. Eh,
               anda talking ofa da pies, I fancy I coulda eat one!
               (takes one off the pile he has collected and eats it
               greedily) Bellissima! Deliciosa! Lots a da gravy!
               (he suddenly discovers a long hair, views it with
               puzzlement and winds it round his finger) Some-
               body's been combing their hair. I no thinka thata
               pie is a nice one. (he puts part of the eaten pie
               back and takes another) Thatsa better ... buta no
               ... Whata have we here? A bone? No, a button ...
               and what .. no ... Santa Maria! ... no ... si ....
               it isa ... ugh! A fingernail! How did a fingernail
               come into a pie? Angelo no feel well. (looks around
               nervously) There isa something funny going on here.

               MUSIC 12 Something Funny Going on Here

ANGELO   There's something strange
               In this place.
               I sense there's danger
               In this place,
               I somehow fear
               Evil is near.
               Isa something funny going on here

               (Lights dim and several GHOSTS appear, including that
               of ALONZO, who looks very put out at the company
               he is keeping.)

GHOST 1   I came 'ere for an 'aircut.
               She popped me in 'er pastry.
               You 'ave me in your 'and there,
               I 'ope you find me tasty!

               (ANGELO drops the pie he's holding.)

GHOST 2   I was Todd's first victim,
                   They used to call me Sidney.
                   'E made me into meat pies,
                   Now I'm steak and kidney!

                   (Apart from ALONZO the GHOSTS all join up to do
                   a jolly cockney-style knees-up dance to the chorus.)

ALL   Lor' luv a duck, sir. Oh, cor blimey!
                   I wish I'd let me beard grow. I wish I'd been wise.
                   What a way to end up - as perishin' pie meat -
                   This homicidal barber cuts his clients down to pies.

GHOST 3   She made me into baked meat
                   And sold me to me wife.
                   She said she'd never 'ad such
                   Indigestion in 'er life!

GHOST 4   We wanted our revenge so
                   We took a tip from 'amlet.
                   We've given you the info
                   But do you understand yet?

ALL   Lor' luv a duck, sir. Oh, cor blimey!
                   As a barber and a butcher he'll be numbered with
                                                         the best.
                   We may have 'ad to end up as perishin' pie meat
                   But when he slits your throat it is a cut above the
                                                         chest!

ANGELO   Dread apparitions
                   I'm on my knees.
                   Grant me remission,
                   Don't kill me please.
                   I somehow fear
                   My end isa near.
                   Isa something funny going on here!

ALONZO   We'd like to see his capture,
                   We cannot rest without it.
                   It's not that we are spiteful -
                   But we feel cut up about it!

GHOST 6   So now it's up to you, son,

We hope you'll lend a hand.
They might think us insubstantial
If we took the witness stand!

(For the final chorus all the GHOSTS including
ALONZO - albeit reluctantly - join in the dance.)

ALL Lor' luv a duck, sir, Oh, cor blimey!
After what he did to us we never can forgive him.
What a way to end up as perishin' pie meat!
If you ask him why he'll tell you IT'S TO CUT THE
          COST OF LIVING!

(GHOSTS exeunt L and R dancing. ANGELO hides
his head, quaking.)

ANGELO These are da murdered ghosts come to aska for
their bodies - and they are amade into da pies!
Plis, it no me! I no know what happen! (looks up
nervously) Oh da holy saints be praised. They are
gone.

off

(The wall behind him starts to open. He screams
and runs out USR. TOBIAS appears knocking bricks
out of the wall and climbs in carrying a sailor hat.)

TOBIAS At last I fancy I have got to the bottom of the mystery.
This passage connects Mr Todd's barber shop with
next door, and here he must dispose of his victims -
but this is the cellar of Mrs Lovett's Pie Shop. She
too must have a part in this murderous business -
and murder is indeed the word! I have discovered,
in the cellar of Todd's shop, this hat belonging to
the sailor whom Todd shaved this morning. He has
not returned to claim it. (sniffs) I fear he never
will. I shall search here in Mrs Lovett's cellar for
further evidence. I am resolved to bring this murderer to justice. (looks behind table) Merciful
Heavens! (looks down again and then steps to
the front of the stage) The very man of whom I
spoke! The handsome sailor who visited the shop
today - dead! (sniffs) His naked body lies in yonder
corner. I must be quick. A policeman!

BILLY   (off) Oooooh!

TOBIAS   But hold!   (dashes back to the table, looks
                  down and dashes back to the front of the stage)
                  He stirs!   (dashes back to table and then forward
                  again) He lives! (dashes back and helps BILLY up)
                  Thank heavens!

                  (BILLY's head appears above the back of the table.
                  He is holding it painfully. TOBIAS dashes R and
                  picks up a piece of sacking.)

                  Here, wrap yourself in this until we can restore
                  your uniform to you.

                  (BILLY turns his back on the audience and wraps the
                  sacking round his waist. Every inch of flesh visible
                  is covered with tattoos. As he turns and shows his
                  chest the name 'SUSAN' is clearly visible.)

BILLY   Oh, my head! Thank you, boy.

TOBIAS   You have a great many tattoos, sir.

BILLY   Indeed. I am every inch a sailor.

TOBIAS   Yes, I noticed that. (reading) 'Susan'. (wistfully)
                  Your sweetheart, sir?

BILLY   The most wonderful lady in the world – and I have
                  seen the world, boy. Now, we must act quickly. This
                  evil barber must be brought to justice. I am inclined
                  to challenge him myself. A fight to the death.

TOBIAS   (her admiration growing by the second) You fear not
                  death, sir?

BILLY   Death? No! Since first I trod the Queen's oak he has
                  been about me. I have slept near him, watched near
                  him. He has looked upon my face and saw I shrunk
                  not. In the storm I have heeded him not. In the fury
                  of the battle I have not thought of him – (change of
                  tone) But, quickly, boy, how do we escape from this
                  dingy charnel-house?

TOBIAS   We must return through this wall to Todd's shop.
                From there we can make our way to the Bow Street
                Police Station.

BILLY   But I cannot walk in public dressed like this.

TOBIAS   You are right. You must be dressed more decently.
                Here.

                (She hands him his sailor's hat.)

BILLY   Ah, that's better! Let us waste no time.

                MUSIC 13

TOBIAS   No. We'll go straight after this song.

                Turn Them In

TOBIAS &   We've discovered the construction of this evil oper-
BILLY   ation.
                They must be punished for their direful sin.
                The black history of their murders makes a gruesome
                                            recitation,
                And now we're going to turn them in.

                Turn them, turn them, turn them in.
                We'll be the heroes of the day!
                Turn them, turn them, turn them in.
                We'll show them that their crime can't pay!

TOBIAS   For years they must have murdered and robbed with-
                                          out detection -
BILLY   It's time their business was brought to a stop!
TOBIAS   Their crimes must be reported 'cos the public needs
                                          protection -
BILLY   They'll both be sentenced to the drop!

TOBIAS &   Turn them, turn them, turn them in.
BILLY   We'll be the heroes of the day!
                Turn them, turn them, turn them in.
                We'll show them that their crime can't pay!

                (At the end of the chorus TODD and MRS LOVETT

enter through the wall (USR, creep behind TOBIAS
and BILLY and knock them out.)

TODD &   They've discovered the construction of our evil
MRS LOVETT   operation.
                It was fortunate that we came in.
                It was imperative that we should interrupt their
                                        celebration -
                For they were going to turn us in!

                Turn us, turn us, turn us in!
                They'll be sorry they came here today.
                Turn us, turn us, turn us in,
                We'll show them that our crime can pay!

                (They repeat the chorus doing a celebratory dance.)

MRS LOVETT   They know our secret, Mr Todd. We shall have to
                dispose of them.   (draws finger across her throat)

TODD   No, no, Mrs Lovett. Simply tie them up. There
                are other ways of silencing them.

MRS LOVETT   Other ways?

TODD   I·have a very good friend ....

                (MRS LOVETT laughs uproariously.)

                ..... (scowling) I repeat. I have a very good
                friend by the name of Mr Napoleon Bedlam. He is
                the warden of the public asylum at Peckham.

MRS LOVETT   The madhouse in Peckham?

TODD   Exactly so.

MRS LOVETT   Of what use is a madhouse keeper to us?

TODD   (laughing hysterically) Do you not see? Shortly he
                will have two more inmates. (starts tying up BILLY)

MRS LOVETT   (tying up TOBIAS)   I see but can we trust him?

TODD

(aside) You, my friend, cannot trust me.   A few
shillings will be sufficient to stop his mouth.   Right,
quickly now.   Take the boy.   I will deal with the
sailor.

(They drag the unfortunate BILLY and TOBIAS off
DSL.   ANGELO appears from the bakehouse USR,
and exit   through   wall into TODD's shop.)

BLACKOUT

Scene 3   The Madhouse at Peckham

(The Madhouse is a dark and dismal place, with
doors DSL, USL and USR.   A large substantial
table DSR on which there is a large padlocked box.
On the wall USC is the inscription 'QUIS CUSTODIET
IPSOS CUSTODES?' The table also has an enormous
book lying on it, and NAPOLEON BEDLAM sitting at
it. He opens the book and scribbles in it. Then he
unlocks the box and counts the contents - it is full of
gold coins.)

BEDLAM

How pleasant it is to hear the sound of gold.   The
very word is music. Gold. Gold. Gold. Gold.
(stands in excitement) Gold. I love it! I want more.
Gold! Ha ha ha ha. (pauses and notices audience)
This is a madhouse..... I know what you're thinking,
You think I am mad. I am the keeper of this establishment. There is no one here who would dare to
call me mad. No, indeed. The inmates know me.
They fear to arouse my anger. They know better than
to annoy me. They know that here I have complete
power over them. The law cannot protect them here.
Within these walls I control all. Supreme power is
mine! Ha ha ha ha! (as his hysteria increases he
climbs onto the table) No one dare challenge my
authority. I am like a god! Indeed to these miserable creatures I am a god. A god almighty. Ha ha ha
ha ha ha!

(As BEDLAM jumps up and down on the table screaming, so TODD enters USR behind him. Aware that

BEDLAM does not realise he is in the room TODD
coughs. BEDLAM turns and is highly embarrassed
by his appearance. He climbs down from the table.)

Mr Sweeney Todd, I think, if my memory don't de-
ceive me?

TODD   You are right, Napoleon Bedlam. I believe I am not
            easily forgotten by those who have once seen me.

BEDLAM   True, sir. You are not easily forgotten. What can
            I do for you now?

TODD   I am rather unfortunate with my boys. I have two
            here who have shown such decided symptoms of
            insanity that it becomes, I regret to say, absolutely
            necessary to place them under your care.

BEDLAM   Indeed? Do they rave?

TODD   Oh yes they do, and about the most absurd nonsense
            in the world. To hear them one would really think
            that, instead of being one of the most humane of men,
            I was, in point of fact, an absolute murderer.

BEDLAM   A murderer?

TODD   Could anything be more absurd than such an accusa-
            tion?

BEDLAM   For how long do you think that this malady will con-
            tinue?

TODD   I will pay for twelve months but I do not think, be-
            tween you and I, that the case will last anything like
            so long. I think they will die like Simkins - suddenly!

            (They both laugh madly.)

BEDLAM   I shouldn't wonder if they did. You may as well
            introduce me to your patients at once.

TODD   I shall have great pleasure in showing them to you.
            (calls off) Mrs Lovett, would you bring in the victims

er, the patients, please?

(MRS LOVETT enters USR leading BILLY and TOBIAS still tied up.)

BEDLAM   Ah, I see that they are quite young.

TODD   Yes, more's the pity.

BEDLAM'   On the contrary, they will be most popular with the audience.

MRS LOVETT   (looking at the audience) With the audience?

TODD   Not that audience.

BEDLAM   No, indeed, ma'am.

MRS LOVETT   What audience then?

TODD   Mr Bedlam raises money for the upkeep of this establishment by allowing the public to visit the asylum - for a small charge.

BEDLAM   The public have a great curiosity on the subject of madness. We try to satisfy that curiosity. If we also make a little money, heh, heh, so much the better!

MRS LOVETT   You mean the public just come in and watch the lunatics?

TODD   In a way. But they do not see them simply running wild. Mr Bedlam trains them.

MRS LOVETT   Trained lunatics?

BEDLAM   Perhaps you would understand better if I were to give you a sample of their performance.

TODD   Oh, no, no. Do not put yourself to such trouble.

BEDLAM   No trouble, sir. (rings bell) They will be here directly.

TODD   (to MRS LOVETT) You and your questions! Now we
                shall both have to suffer.

                (From the dark door USL a number of half naked,
                ragged, unkempt creatures shamble towards the
                front of the stage. They are lit only by blue lights.
                Some come DSR behind MRS LOVETT who is startled
                and runs to hide behind BEDLAM.)

BEDLAM   There is no need for fear, ma'am. They are per-
                fectly harmless - except for Enoch.

ENOCH   Grrrrrrrr!

BEDLAM   I would introduce you but it would be useless.

MRS LOVETT   Useless? Why?

BEDLAM   Let me demonstrate. (to INMATE 1) Good evening.

INMATE 1   Boots, boots, boots, boots, boots, boots, boots -

BEDLAM   (striking him) Your name?

INMATE 1   I am Napoleon Bonaparte. (strikes a Napoleon pose)

BEDLAM   Indeed? And who told you that?

INMATE 1   God. God told me.

INMATE 2   I did no such thing!

                (INMATES 1 and 2 fight. BEDLAM beats them apart.)

BEDLAM   You see conversation is useless, but there is one way
                in which they can express themselves. My visitors
                usually find it - amusing.

MRS LOVETT   What way is that?

BEDLAM   It is a form of singing ... er ... music.

MRS LOVETT   A form of music?

BEDLAM   I have given it the name of **rock** music.

TODD   Why rock music?

BEDLAM   When **it**'s over you feel like you've been hit by a
              rock! Stand clear, please. I would not like you to
              be injured during the performance. We begin with
              a little mathematics. Right, pay attention, (coughs)
              counting begin.

INMATE 1   One.

INMATE 2   Two.

INMATE 3   Five.

INMATE 4   Eight.

BEDLAM   No, no, no. Again. Counting – begin!

INMATE 1   One.

INMATE 2   One.

BEDLAM   No, two.

INMATE 3   Two.

BEDLAM   No, you're three, he's two.

INMATE 4   He's thirty five if he's a day.

BEDLAM   No, no, NO! (to TODD and MRS LOVETT) This won't
              take a moment. (to INMATES) Repeat after me. One.

INMATES   One.

BEDLAM   Two.

INMATES   Two.

BEDLAM   Three.

INMATES   Three.

BEDLAM	Four.
INMATES	Four.
BEDLAM	Now we're getting somewhere.
INMATES	Now we're getting somewhere.
BEDLAM	(embarrassed) Ha ha ha.
INMATES	Ha ha ha.
BEDLAM	No, no, no.
INMATES	No, no, no.
BEDLAM	Stop it!
INMATES	Stop it!
BEDLAM	I'll thrash the next –
INMATES	I'll thrash the next –

(BEDLAM screams. The INMATES scream. BEDLAM now cunningly remains silent. He walks around the line of INMATES like a sergeant-major.)

BEDLAM	Repeat after me.
INMATES	Repeat after me.
BEDLAM	One, two, three, four.
INMATES	One, two, three, four.
BEDLAM	One, two, three, four.
INMATES	One, two, three, four.
BEDLAM	One, two, three, four.
INMATES	One, two, three, four.

(This last count leads into <u>MUSIC 14</u>   Each INMATE
produces a microphone. They dance frantically.
Coloured lights and a strobe add to the excitement.)

<u>Crazy</u>

INMATES   Look around, see our plight.
               Locked in here out of sight.
               In our padded cells confined,
               We are all out of our minds.

               Pity our misery,
               Victims of society.
               Kept in dungeons here below -
               Every day another show!

               We don't care if they all say we're crazy!
               We don't care if they all say we're crazy!
               We don't care if they all say we're crazy!
               Yeah!

               Every day there's a chance
               To see our madman's dance.
               Every step that we complete
               Jolts our wits into our feet!

               Every day people throng
               To hear our madman's song.
               Looney tunes from every throat
               Paranoia in each note!

               CHORUS

               Wouldn't it break your hearts?
               We are all Bonapartes.
               We, the Emperors of France
               Here are forced to sing and dance.

               But admit that it's true
               We have fun, more than you.
               Pleasures sure from madness grow,
               Which none but we madmen know.

               CHORUS

(During the song TOBIAS and BILLY have been struggling with their ropes. TOBIAS has managed to
remove her gag.)

TOBIAS   (shouting) Sweeney Todd is a murderer and I
                  denounce him!

TODD   You hear him?

BEDLAM   Mad indeed.

MRS LOVETT   Could anyone but a maniac make so absurd an
                  assertion?

BEDLAM   No, it is insanity in its most terrible form. I see
                  I shall have to put him in a strait-waistcoat.

TODD   I'm afraid mild treatment, which I have tried, only
                  irritates the disease. Therefore I must leave you,
                  as a professional, to deal with the case as seems fit.

MRS LOVETT   But time presses on, Mr Todd, and I have no doubt
                  the patients will be properly attended to.

                  (They start to leave, shaking hands with BEDLAM.)

TODD   (to TOBIAS) Ha haaaa! How do you feel now? Do
                  you still think I shall hang or will you die in the cell
                  of a madhouse? (to audience) Do you see, my friends,
                  how evil will always triumph over weak, wishy-washy
                  goodness and kindness? Ha ha haaaaaa!

                  (TODD and MRS LOVETT leave USR.)

BILLY   Ummmm. Urgle, urle, urgle.

                  (BEDLAM removes his gag.)

                  I don't know who you are, sir, but let me beg you to
                  have the house of Sweeney Todd, in Fleet Street,
                  searched and you will find that he is a murderer.

TOBIAS   There are at least a hundred watches, rings, trinkets
                  and other belongings of the unfortunate persons who

have met their deaths through him.

BEDLAM   How uncommonly mad!   (rings the bell - two
                KEEPERS enter) You will take these new inmates
                under your care. They seem extremely unsettled
                and feverish. Shave their heads and put strait-
                waistcoats on them. Let them be conveyed to one
                of the dark, damp cells as too much light will en-
                courage their wild delirium.

BILLY   We will die before we submit to you!

BEDLAM   Then die! For no power can aid you!

TOBIAS   Yes, there is one - Heaven - which fails not to suc-
                cour the helpless and the persecuted.

                (BILLY has been struggling with his ropes, now with
                one mighty bound he is free!)

BILLY   Now, sir, we meet on equal terms. (frees TOBIAS)

BEDLAM   Quickly fools, restrain them.

                (An enormous fight takes place between TOBIAS,
                BILLY and BEDLAM and the two KEEPERS. At first
                the INMATES just watch.)

BILLY   Come my friends! This is your chance to be free
                from this vile and accursed prison.

                (The INMATES join in the fight carrying off BEDLAM
                and the two KEEPERS USL.)

                Free! Let us go quickly - Bow Street!

                (TOBIAS and BILLY exeunt USR.)

Scene 4   Fleet Street

(MRS LOVETT's Pie Shop USL, TODD's Barber Shop
USR. TODD and MRS LOVETT enter DSR cross stage
sniggering and enter the Pie Shop. They are followed

a moment later by the POLICE CONSTABLE.)

CONSTABLE   Evening all. I think I hear footsteps. (pause –
              nothing happens, he looks into wings and repeats
              louder:) I THINK I HEAR FOOTSTEPS!

              (FOOZLE, TOMMY and ORLANDO run on stage from
              one side, BILLY and TOBIAS from the other. BILLY
              is now fully dressed in what ever he has persuaded
              the INMATES and TOBIAS to give him.)

FOOZLE   (to CONSTABLE) Come quickly!

CONSTABLE   What seems to be the trouble?

              (They all gabble incomprehensibly for ten seconds
              finishing in perfect unison:)

              Just as I thought, but ...?

              (They gabble again. ORLANDO bounds around madly.)

              Ah, I see. Does that mean ....?

              (They gabble again ending together with:)

ALL   The Pie Shop!   (all point at the door)

CONSTABLE   The unspeakable fiend!

FOOZLE   What are we to do?

BILLY   A brilliant idea!

FOOZE   Yes?

TOBIAS   Yes?

BILLY   That's what we need – a brilliant idea.

CONSTABLE   In a case like this there is only one thing to do –

ALL   What?

CONSTABLE   Stand back! With one blast on this whistle I will
                 summon .... the Dwarf Squad!

ALL   The Dwarf Squad?

CONSTABLE   Observe!

                 (He blows the whistle. Six POLICEMEN march on
                 and line up. They can either be the six smallest
                 members of the cast or the six largest - on their
                 knees with dummy shoes attached!)

ALL   Amazing!

FOOZLE   It's a sort of teeny weeny Sweeney.

POLICEMEN   Evenin' all, 'ello, 'ello, 'ello. What's all this 'ere
                 then? Mind how you go.

TOBIAS   (whispers) But why are they all dwarves?

CONSTABLE   They're specially trained for dealing with low crimi-
                 nals.

FOOZLE   Little doubt.

TOMMY   Small wonder.

CONSTABLE   Dwarf Constables, atten - SHUN!

                 (They come smartly to attention.)

                 At the double .... wait for it ... to the Barber's
                 Shop!

                 (The CONSTABLE heads DSL, all the others rush off
                 stage R. The CONSTABLE stops and looks back. He
                 blows his whistle and signals to them to follow him.
                 The others all appear again and dash across the stage
                 knocking the CONSTABLE over and trampling on him.
                 He gets up shakily and staggers after them. Finally
                 after a lot of whistle blowing off stage the CONSTABLE
                 leads the POLICEMEN, TOMMY, BILLY, TOBIAS,FOO-
                 ZLE and ORLANDO USR and into TODD's shop.)

Scene 5 The Bakehouse in MRS LOVETT's cellar

(TODD and MRS LOVETT are discovered in violent
argument.)

MRS LOVETT   My mind is made up, Mr Todd. I will no longer have
              anything to do with this evil business. I cannot sleep
              without dreaming of our countless victims, our bru-
              tal crimes. Horrible nightmares!

TODD   It is too late for you to be troubled with a conscience.
              (aside) The time has come to dispose of this pom-
              pous pie-maker.

MRS LOVETT   May God forgive me for my sins! (aside) One final
              murder and I shall be safe.   (shows the audience
              her hidden knife)

TODD   Come, come. We have been friends these many
              years. Let us not quarrel now.

MRS LOVETT   You are right, of course, Mr Todd. It is as you say,
              Mr Todd, friends, the greatest of friends.

TODD   Thick as thieves, Mrs Lovett.

MRS LOVETT   Oh yes, certainly, Mr Todd .... thick, Mr Todd ....
              very thick.

              (They move to opposite sides of the stage as MUSIC 15
              begins:)

Thick As Thieves

MRS LOVETT   You're my oldest comrade, Sweeney,
              Why I'm almost like your wife.
              I'll be very pleased to see you
              On the sharp end of my knife!

              (She throws knife at TODD, it misses and sticks in the
              wall with a thud. TODD does not notice.)

TODD   My dear companion, I am yours,
              My inseparable aide.

Her friendship may decline, of course,
When she feels my razor blade!

(He turns swinging his razor violently at the spot
where he thinks MRS LOVETT is standing. She isn't
there - he misses, spins and falls over. The razor
skids away out of reach.)

BOTH   Thick as thieves,
                Thick as thieves.
                We're the greatest of friends. It'd make you sick,
                Although you may think that thieves are thick
                Not we -
                We're thick, thick, thick, thick,
                Thick, thick, thick, thick,
                Thick, thick, thick, thick,
                Thick as thieves!

MRS LOVETT   I have often heard the saying,
                'A true friend is hard to beat'.
                I know what kind of game he's playing -
                You look tired, take a seat!

                (She picks up a chair to smash on TODD's head, but
                as she swings it it falls apart and she is left holding
                a single leg. She smiles sweetly at TODD.)

TODD   My friend, your words have touched me,
                We'll be comrades until death -
                Which in her case will come shortly,
                She seems somehow out of breath!

                (TODD has, he thinks, thrown a cord around MRS
                LOVETT's neck and is fiercely strangling her. In fact
                the cord is around a hatstand. MRS LOVETT walks in
                to TODD's line of vision.He drops the cord and smiles.)

BOTH   CHORUS

TODD   You have a beautiful singing voice, Mrs Lovett.

MRS LOVETT   Why thank you, Mr Todd.

TODD   (pulling out a pistol and shooting MRS LOVETT who

falls to the ground, dead) They say the Devil has
all the best tunes. He will be pleased to see you!
She is gone - gone - and not a witness to the deed!

ANGELO   (sticking his head through wall USR) Excepta me!

TODD   (not noticing ANGELO) Dead men tell no tales! I
am free! I am free! Ha ha haaaaaaa! Now let the
furnace consume the body as it would wheaten straw
and destroy all evidence of my guilt in this as it has
in my manifold deeds of blood.

(He goes USC to MRS LOVETT's body, putting down
the gun near the wall USR. ANGELO reaches in and
picks it up whilst TODD is recoiling from the body.)

Those eyes! She stares at me - even in death she
accuses me, but take courage. The body must be
removed.

(He approaches it again, head averted. ANGELO
enters USR unseen.)

ANGELO   Sweeney Todd! I accuse you of murder!

TODD   (screams) Oh save me! The dead accuse me!
Mercy! I cry mercy! (turns and sees that it is
ANGELO) It is the Italian boy! You think to frighten
me, boy. I will deal swiftly with you.

(He moves towards ANGELO, who points the gun at
him. TODD stops in his tracks.)

(smiling) Come, come, Angelo amico, is it to be
war or peace between us?

ANGELO   War! War to the last! War until I see you, signore,
placed in da felon's dock anda sentenced bya da judge.

TODD   Be prudent. Remember, I am now rich.

ANGELO   But your reign will soon be over. What will your position be, do you think, when the world knows all?

TODD   (advancing) You foolish urchin I will -

ANGELO   Stand back or I willa shoot.

                        (TODD advances, ANGELO pulls the trigger but the
                        gun is empty. TODD laughs and dives for him. At
                        this moment, just in the nick of time, the door DSL
                        bursts open and in march the CONSTABLE, POLICE -
                        MEN, TOMMY, BILLY, TOBIAS, FOOZLE and ORLAN-
                        DO.)

CONSTABLE   Sweeney Todd, I arrest you in the name of Her Impe-
                        rial Majesty Queen Victoria. Restrain him!

                        (The POLICEMEN grab TODD. He is handcuffed to
                        the tiniest.)

TOBIAS   Now Sweeney Todd you shall hang for your wicked
                        crimes!

BILLY   You were a fool to think that you could escape.

FOOZLE   Now Londoners will be safe from your cut-throat
                        razor.

TOMMY   All thanks to the dwarf squad.

ANGELO   I thinka your British Policemen are awonderful.

CONSTABLE   Why, thank you. We do our best, you know.

TODD   You think to arrest me? You will have to catch me
                        first!

                        (With this he dashes off through the audience heading
                        for the back exit, dragging with him the POLICEMAN
                        to whom he is handcuffed. There is an enormous
                        chase through the audience, everybody shouting,
                        whistles going off, bells ringing. The CONSTABLE
                        fires a gun. Sirens and strobe lighting all add to the
                        confusion. When all the cast have exited at the back
                        of the audience TODD reappears on stage free from
                        his handcuffs. He hides under the table USL. Seconds
                        later his pursuers appear. They look all around.)

BILLY   He has escaped.

TOBIAS   We have let him slip from our grasp.

                 (The table is walking slowly across the stage.)

FOOZLE   I think not. Look! (points at table)

                 (They all stare at the table. BILLY and TOMMY
                 stand on either side of it. They lift the table off
                 TODD who continues to crawl across the stage. The
                 POLICEMEN grab him.)

CONSTABLE   Take him away.

                 (TODD and POLICEMEN carry MRS LOVETT's body off.)

TOBIAS   What will happen to him, sir?

CONSTABLE   Justice will take its course.

BILLY   We shall have to wait for news.

NEWSBOY   (entering DSL and crossing stage) Extra! Extra!
                 Sweeney Todd to hang! Extra! Extra! (exit DSR)

TOMMY   A fitting end for such a criminal.

                 (The POLICEMEN bring back TODD covered in chains
                 and with a ball and chain around his ankle. He weeps
                 and falls to his knees.)

TODD   Oh woe is me! May Heaven forgive me for my dark
                 and foul deeds. I feared it would come to this and all
                 through accursed gold, for which men sell their souls
                 and barter their eternal salvation. REPENT! Repent!
                 Truly I repent! Spare me! Spare my life, I beg you.
                 Will no one speak for me? Just one word?

                 (They all turn their backs on him. NEWSBOY returns.)

NEWSBOY   Extra! Extra! Queen pardons Sweeney Todd!

ALL   (turning back) WHAT?!

NEWSBOY   d.

FOOZLE

VICTORIA   atever we like, you
                                       ＿ѕn. We are the Queen.
                                   ＿ιamation. 'It is our wish that Mr
                           ＿ney Todd, having been found guilty of twenty-
                   seven separate murders shall not be hanged. He
                   shall be imprisoned for life ....'

TODD   (delighted) I am spared! Thank the Lord!

VICTORIA   Thank who?

TODD   Thank you, your Majesty.

VICTORIA   That's better ...... 'he shall be imprisoned for life
                   in the madhouse of Mr Napoleon Bedlam at Peckham.'

TODD   (his face falling) What? No! Hang me! Hang me!

VICTORIA   Be quiet,you ungrateful man. Mr Bedlam has sent -
                   under guard of course - some of his inmates to wel-
                   come you to their number.

                   (The INMATES rush on DSL and surround TODD.)

TODD   No, no, anything but this.

ENOCH   One, two, three, four.

TODD   I am not mad. Ask them. (gestures to the audience)
                   They will tell you that I'm not mad. Tell them! Tell
                   them!

AUDIENCE   (encouraged by TOBIAS) Oh yes you are.

TODD   Oh no I'm not.

AUDIENCE   Oh yes you are.

TODD   Oh no I'm not.

AUDIENCE.   Oh yes you are.

TODD   All right, don't start enjoying yourselves now.
             We've nearly finished.

ENOCH   (hitting TODD) One, two, three, four.

             (The INMATES take TODD USL.)

VICTORIA   And now we must reward those who have brought
             this monster to justice. You may all have an OBE.
             (she produces a bag and flings medals in every
             direction)

BILLY   I must return at once to Kent to marry my sweet-
             heart, Susan.

TOBIAS   (crossing to BILLY) Alas what will now become of
             me? I have no master and no money. And, alas, my
             name isn't Susan.   (takes off her cap revealing
             her long hair)

ALL   GASP!

             (BILLY stands amazed. They look into each others
             eyes, romantic violins are heard - sound effects.)

BILLY   You're ... you're .....

TOBIAS   Yes.

BILLY   No....

ALL   YES!

BILLY   Why you're beautiful!

             (They walk towards each other and stand face to face.)

             My darling. Come to my farm, marry me and let us
             live happily ever after.

TOBIAS   Oh yes my darling.

VICTORIA   One moment! What about Susan?

BILLY   Susan who?

(BILLY and TOBIAS kiss.)

FOOZLE   Come, Orlando, our master is dead.

(ORLANDO howls.)

(brightening) But we have his secrets. His skills will live on in me. I too shall astound the crowned heads of Europe. (looks at VICTORIA and produces a pack of cards) Your Majesty, pick a card - any card.

(FOOZLE and VICTORIA go USR and continue with the card trick.)

ANGELO   That leavesa only me. I have no one, nothing. Only my holy medal of Saint Peter. (on chain round his neck)

TOMMY   (coming forward and inspecting the medal)   Boy, where did you get this medal?

ANGELO   I have had it, signore, all my life, since I was a bambino in Napoli. My mamma she tell me that my father, he leave it for me. He die before I was born.

TOMMY   I had a .. a ... a wife in Naples some twelve years since. I was forced to leave her. I left her and my unborn child the only wealth I possessed - a silver medal of Saint Peter.

(Everybody looks at everybody else!)

ANGELO   Father!

TOMMY   My son!

(They embrace.)

ANGELO   I have found a home.

TOMMY   And wealth. That medal is of great value.

BILLY   But even better than your new found home, even better than your new found wealth you have a - New Found Land! Angelo, my shipmate Tommy is your father. You realise what this means?

ANGELO   It cannot be true.

BILLY   Yes - Angelo - you are BRITISH!

ANGELO   It is all too good to be true!

(They all cheer.)

MUSIC 16   Queen and Empire   (reprise)

ALL   In Heaven's eye who can deny
That Britain stands and stands alone?
In pride of place the supreme race.
All others are in shadow thrown.

On yonder height what golden light
Triumphant shines and shines alone?
Unrivall'd blaze the nation's gaze
'tis not the sun, 'tis Britain's throne.

On which the sun,   on which the sun,
On which the sun,   on which the sun,
On which the sun,   the sun, the sun,
The sun, the sun,   the sun, the sun,
On which the bright and glorious,
Queen Victorious,
Bright and glorious,
Queen Victorious
SU-UN
NEVER SETS!

FOOZLE   (dashing to the front of the stage) But wait! In mem ory of my poor dead master I must complete his most famous illusion. (to VICTIM 2) If you would step up here once more, sir. Most kind, sir. Most kind!

(VICTIM 2 returns to the stage. FOOZLE fills the

hat with goo from the jug. This time there are no
interruptions and VICTIM 2 puts the hat on. With a
dramatic gesture FOOZLE lifts the hat and the goo
covers VICTIM 2's head and face. FOOZLE is a
little aghast and edges away:)

Ah ... er ... yes, well ..... congratulations. This
half a bacon sandwich is yours!

(With a shriek of fury VICTIM 2 chases FOOZLE off
the stage, through the audience and out of the back
door. Meanwhile on stage the INMATES bring TODD
forward. ENOCH whispers in the ear of the CON-
STABLE.)

CONSTABLE   He says that they have something to show us.

TOBIAS   What can it be?

               (ENOCH whispers to CONSTABLE.)

CONSTABLE   They have been educating Sweeney Todd.

TOBIAS   Let us see what they have taught him.

ENOCH   (to TODD) One, two, three, four.

               (TODD remains obstinately silent.)

               ONE, TWO, THREE, FOUR!

               (ENOCH raises his fist at TODD.)

TODD   (miserably) One, two, three, four.

               (MUSIC 17 crashes in. Everybody, including VICTORIA,
               dances madly. Strobe and coloured lighting effects.)

               Crazy!   (reprise)

ALL   Every day there's a chance
               To see our madman's dance.
               Every step that we complete
               Jolts our wits into our feet!

Every day people throng
To hear our madman's song.
Looney tunes from every throat -
Paranoia in each note!

Don't you know that everyone is crazy!
Don't you know that everyone is crazy!
Don't you know that everyone is crazy -
Yeah!

BLACKOUT

CURTAIN

MUSIC 18   National Anthem

PRODUCTION NOTES

STYLE

Although the play parodies the Victorian melodramas on which it is based, it is full of anachronisms and contains musical numbers far removed from any Victorian style. Therefore there should be no sign that the cast are anything but serious in their performances. If the actors appear to be sending themselves up, the humour will be much diluted.

STAGING

The Fleet Street scenes need minimal scenery, although a doorway must be suggested - preferably two. If tabs are available these can be used for the Fleet Street scenes, allowing the other sets to be prepared out of sight of the audience, although this is by no means essential. The stage plans for the sets as described in this script are included at the back of the book. There is no reason why an excellent production should not be based on just the few basic essential pieces of furniture required by the script - doorways, TODD's chair, tables and chairs for the Gin Palace, a few blocks to represent cellar walls and the exploding pie machine. If more elaborate facilities are available then there are opportunities to create full sets - particularly useful for the climax of the Gin Palace scene and for the gruesome cellar in which most of Act Two takes place.

EQUIPMENT AND EFFECTS

There are several ways in which TODD's chair can be constructed:

a) A simple solution is to place a chair on castors which can be pulled from behind through a curtained section of 'wall'.

b) A simple revolving panel can be constructed. The chair and a section of 'wall' are attached to a small platform which is spun from the rear.

c) The most effective method is to attach the chair to an L-shaped wooden base which is hinged to the floor of the stage. As the chair is tipped backwards the 'floor' comes up to fill the gap through which the chair has disappeared.

d) The coward's way out is to fade the lights and let the actor exit in the normal way in the darkness. This is the least fun and there will always be someone who can see the supposedly murdered body walking out on his own two legs!

Version (c) is illustrated overleaf.

Method 'C'

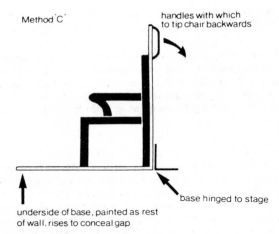

handles with which
to tip chair backwards

underside of base, painted as rest
of wall, rises to conceal gap

base hinged to stage

TODD's Chair (c)

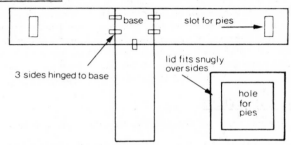

base

slot for pies

3 sides hinged to base

lid fits snugly
over sides

hole
for
pies

The Exploding Pie Machine (Exploded Plan!)

The first essential is a good loud BANG! Maroons of various sizes
are available from theatrical suppliers and are not expensive. Use
the biggest one you dare! Properly handled they are harmless!
The machine itself is simply constructed and foolproof in operation.
To a base large enough for the OPERATOR to stand on are hinged the
front and sides of the machine – it has no back. They are held up and
together by a lid which slots over the top of them. It is like a biscuit-
tin lid but with a hole in the middle through which the ingredients can
be thrown in and the pies thrown out. When the OPERATOR gives the
lid a quick hard blow it should fly upwards, allowing the three 'walls'
to fall outwards. The sides SL and SR should have holes in them
through which the pies can be fired.

The pies themselves can be made from cardboard, plaster of Paris,

foam rubber etc. The essential thing to remember is that the ones
that are likely to hit anyone should be as light as possible and the
ones that are actually going to be eaten should be edible! For the
stack of pies (P.54) use foam rubber cut-outs with a string running
through the middle, holding them together.

For the 'Thick as Thieves' number a collapsing chair is required.
An ordinary wooden chair should be demolished and re-assembled
using brown sticky paper. This is just strong enough to hold the
chair together as it is lifted but it will tear allowing the chair to fall
apart when it is jerked sharply.
This song also requires a knife to stick in the wall. Two knives are
needed   here. MRS LOVETT pretends to throw the real knife, con-
cealing it as she does so. Seconds later the second 'dummy' knife
appears to stick in the wall. It is in fact just a handle and a small
section of blade fitted into a piece of the 'wall' to lie flush with it.
A wire is attached at the rear and when this is pulled sharply the
knife snaps into position. There should also be an appropriate
thumping sound. The timing of this effect is vital and it needs to be
carefully rehearsed. When it is performed properly the effect is
startling!

The ALONZO/FOOZLE hat trick is explained in the text.

LIGHTING

One or two spots are useful if other lighting is limited. For the madhouse song as many disco-style effects as the budget can stand should
be used. Rapidly changing coloured filters in the follow-spots as they
sweep randomly about are very effective.

CAST

The size of the CHORUS (CITIZENS, NEWSPAPER BOYS, GIN PALACE
CUSTOMERS, LUNATICS, POLICEMEN, GHOSTS etc) can vary accor-
ding to the wishes (and energy) of the producer. We suggest a mini-
mum of six but,generally speaking,the more the merrier. At least
two separate groups of chorus singers will be necessary.

The play was originally performed by an all male cast but in this
edition it has been adapted for a mixed one. If an all male cast is
used   to perform the play the following alterations should be made:

a) MRS LOVETT becomes MR LOVETT. This involves only a few small
and obvious changes in the dialogue and lyrics.

b) QUEEN VICTORIA becomes a drag role, as in the original production.

c) The following smaller parts can be played equally well by actors
or actresses - PICKPOCKET, CITIZENS OF LONDON, GIN PALACE

CUSTOMERS, MADHOUSE INMATES, NEWSPAPER SELLERS, CHILDREN
in the Gin Palace, PIE-MACHINE OPERATOR, HECKLER, GHOSTS and
ORLANDO.

d) The theatrical tradition whereby the part of TOBIAS is played by
a girl can be abandoned and the part played straight. The necessary
cuts and alternative lines can be found below:

Page 5

NEWSBOY   Well, I wish you luck, mate.

            (NEWSBOY leaves. TOBIAS starts to sob loudly.
            TODD walks out of his shop and strikes him.)

TODD   Be quiet!. You squealing bundle of rags.
            (continue with text)

Page 80

TOBIAS   ...... I have no master and no money.

BILLY   I return at once to Kent to marry my sweetheart,
            Susan. You may come and work on the farm with
            us. You shall be like a son to me.

TOBIAS   Father! (goes to BILLY)

FOOZLE   Come, Orlando, our master is dead.
            (continue with text)

PROPS LIST

ACT I

CHARACTER	PROPERTY	SCENE
NEWSBOYS	newspapers	1
	'MEANWHILE' notice	1
PICKPOCKET	2 watches and 2 wallets	1
TOBIAS	bundle on a stick	1
	banknote	1
	bowl of shaving soap and brush	2
TODD	articles of Apprenticeship and pen	1
	razors	2
	piles of clothes BILLY's and ALONZO's	2
	£40 in banknotes	3
	'RESERVED' sign	3
ALONZO	a case marked 'THE AMAZING ALONZO' in it:	1
	2 bowler hats, a jug of 'disgusting, sticky	
	goo', a gold sovereign	
FOOZLE	a dog collar and lead	1
	half a bacon sandwich	1
	'THE AMAZING ALONZO' case	2
TOMMY	parrot on shoulder	1
BILLY	string of pearls	2
GROVEL	dog bowl, mug of cocoa and tray	3
GILBERT	walking stick	3
CUSTOMERS	glasses, mugs, large jugs labelled 'GIN'	3

ACT II

NEWSBOY	newspapers	5
TOBIAS	sailor's hat	2
TODD	razor, cord and pistol (not revolver)	5
	ball and chain	5
FOOZLE	'THE AMAZING ALONZO' case with contents	5
PIE MACHINE OPERATOR	pies	2

MRS LOVETT	notice 'NEXT BATCH OF PIES READY IN TEN MINUTES'	1
	pies	1
	bag of flour	2
	'human leg and other items' on a tray	2
	knife	5
ANGELO	pie (hot)	2
	stack of pies	2
	jug of water	2
	silver medal of Saint Peter	5
BILLY	a piece of sacking	2
BEDLAM	a large padlocked box full of gold coins	3
	a large ledger book	3
	a handbell	3
POLICEMEN	guns and handcuffs	5
VICTORIA	a bag full of medals	5

****

<u>STAGE PLAN</u>

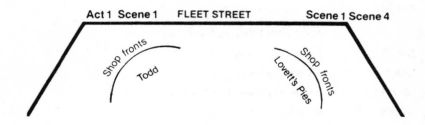

Act 1 Scene 1   FLEET STREET   Scene 1 Scene 4

Shop fronts   Todd   Lovett's Pies   Shop fronts

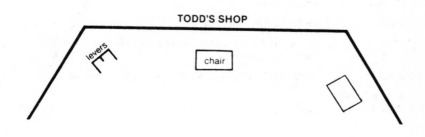

TODD'S SHOP

levers   chair

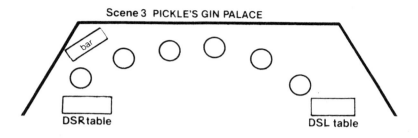

Scene 3 PICKLE'S GIN PALACE

bar

DSR table

DSL table

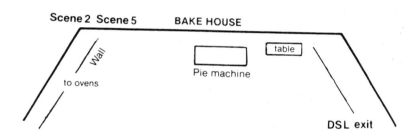

Scene 2 Scene 5 BAKE HOUSE

Wall

to ovens

Pie machine

table

DSL exit

MAD HOUSE AT PECKHAM

banner on wall

USL exit

Printed in Great Britain by Redwood Books,
Trowbridge, Wiltshire